Praise for *The Practical Empath*

"If you enjoy a good read, full of helpful suggestions and remarkable insight into being an empath, then this book *The Practical Empath* is for you. This fascinating book is informative while being written in typical Cathy Kane style. It gives you a window of understanding as to who an empath is, a brief synopsis about energy and how it works, shielding techniques, how much input is too much, and so much more. Cathy is an amazing empath who has helped countless people to learn how to deal with this wonderful, however sometimes daunting gift. This book makes a great read for the novice and experienced empaths alike. With Cathy's guidance, you will learn how to cope with being an empath, and, hopefully, you will get as much, if not more, out of her book *The Practical Empath* as I did. Happy reading."

    -Delilah Kieffer, spiritualist and psychic

"A wonderfully informative and well-explained detail of being a psychic empath. Catherine's book *The Practical Empath* is written with the sympathetic view of a friend reaching out to help and inform other. The author's personality shines through. Truly a gifted view."

    -Alexis Doyle, host of "Cauldron of Knowledge" Radio
       on liveparanormal.com/History FM

"This book is for everyone. It's easy to see how a book with practical advice and even exercises can help empaths themselves; but it's also for people like parents and friends of empaths who have to deal with loved ones who might otherwise be thought of as "difficult" or "high maintenance". Guess what- not only were you "born this way", there's nothing wrong with you (or them)! Even better, this book helps you understand how to deal with way you, or your friends, are, so that it can become the blessing that it can be when you understand. Even those less empathic can benefit from the wisdom collected by someone who has personally turned her empathy into a blessing for all those around her."

    -Tchipakkan , professional psychic and metaphysical speaker

"I absolutely loved this book! I read this looking for useful tips I could use with my empathic child, and was surprised and delighted at how much of the material I could use myself. A definite must-have in any psychic or magic user's library."

    -Morgan Daimler, author of *By Land, Sea and Sky*

And also for Catherine's previous book
Adventures in Palmistry,

"The information in this book is clear, concise, hits the pertinent points of palmistry, and immediately lets you start practicing your craft."
    -Adam Latin, professional palmist

"Having read over 50 books on palmistry, I can say that Cathy not only gives good solid information, but also makes it more accessible for a beginner than any other. Her homey style is like chatting to a friend who knows what she's talking about. She also shares wonderful techniques in <u>Adventures</u> that I've seen in no other books."
    -Virginia Fair Richard-Taylor,
        student and practitioner of palmistry for over 40 years

"Ms. Kane is not only a talented palm reader, but a talented writer as well. She explains the concepts and techniques clearly, and with a sense of humor."
    -Lois Fitzpatrick, leader, East Kingdom Soothsayer's Guild,
        an organization studying
            the methods and history of psychic readings

The
Practical
Empath

Also by Catherine Kane –

Adventures in Palmistry

For more information, please visit Foresight Publications at
www.ForesightYourPsychic.com

The Practical Empath

Surviving and Thriving As a Psychic Empath

by Catherine Kane

Foresight Publications
Wallingford, Ct.

The Practical Empath ©Sept2011 by Catherine Kane

From the Author

There are many exercises and meditations in this book that can help you to develop the skills you need to make your psychic empathy a gift to you. You may wish to read them and do the exercises from memory, or you may prefer to record them to play back while you visualize.

If you record the exercises, please remember to leave some time between each statement in order to have time to visualize.

You have the author's permission to record these exercises for your own personal use in meditation, but, if you wish to record them for any commercial purposes whatsoever, you must obtain written permission from the author. All rights to this work are reserved exclusively to the author unless otherwise specified by written contract.

ISBN 978-0-9846951-9-5

Foresight Publications
Wallingford, CT.

This book is dedicated to

Tchipakkan

With much appreciation for

her help and support on this book

and in life in general,

And also in anticipation of seeing

her own book come out soon…

Acknowledgements

One name goes on the cover, but it takes more people than that to bring a book into the world. I want to acknowledge and thank some of those people now.

To all of the empaths I've had the honor to coach, teach or advise on their gifts. Every journey is unique. I've learned a lot from you, and hope I've helped on your journey, too.

To Adam Latin, who said "I thought you were writing the book about empaths…" before I'd even thought of this; and who helped me clarify what needed to be in it.

To the leaders and members of my writing groups, NaNo Buddies and the Fairfield County Writer's Group, for the encouragement a writer needs to keep on writing.

To Morgan Daimler and Alexis Doyle, for their helpful feedback.

To David Decker, techno-jedi, the right man at the right time with the right idea, who helped the closed doors open.

To Tchipakkan, for continued input and support on my writing, and the example that keeps me moving forwards.

To Delilah Kieffer, for all of your encouragement and belief in myself and my dreams.

And most of all, to my husband Starwolf.

They say that behind every great man stands a woman. Well, behind me stands a great man, who is wise, talented, patient and loving. Without him, this book would not have been written. With him, this woman is a happy and productive author.

Table of Contents

Introduction– 1

One- What is a Psychic Empath (and Am I One?) 3

Two - The Empath and Energy 9

Three- The Empath and the Science of Magick 13

Four- The Ups and Downs of Psychic Empathy 19

Five- A Question of Ethics; and Manners for Psychics 31

Six- Energetic Shields– an Empath's Best Friend 39

Seven- Protecting Your Personal Energy 51

Eight-Separating from Other People's Energy 59

Nine- Energetic House Cleaning- Clearing, Grounding and
     Releasing Unwanted Energy 65

Ten- Keeping Your Energy Positive 91

Eleven- Sorting Out Energy 109

Twelve- The Projective Empath 111

Thirteen- Better Living Through Psychic Empathy 125

Fourteen- The Empath at Work 133

Fifteen- Empathic Children 141

Sixteen-The Personal Touch-
          Psychic Empaths as Friends or Lovers 155

Seventeen- One Journey Ends; Another Begins 163

Biography

Exercises

Are You a Psychic Empath?   5

Building Basic Energetic Shields   39

Energetic Shields Upgrade 42

Light Level Shields 46

Breathing Meditation for Clearing Negative Energy 71

Grounding Out Energy Through a Tree   75

Grounding Energy While Sitting   76

Grounding Energy Through Fire.   79

Grounding Out Negative Energy in the Shower   83

Guided Visualization For Clearing Negative Energy   85

The Emotional Scale 98

Are You a Projective/Radiant Empath?   113

Is Your Child a Psychic Empath?   141

Introduction

Are you uncomfortable in crowds?

When someone whispers angrily, do you feel like they're shouting?

Do you find that the only way you can be happy is make sure that everyone else around you is happy first?

Have you been accused of being "oversensitive"?

If so, you may be a psychic empath;

And this book was written for you.

It's written to help you understand your gift. To overcome the challenges you'll face and to better use the skills that go with your empathy. To learn not just how to survive, but also thrive with your special psychic gift.

And, if you're not a psychic empath, but you work with one, or are raising one, or are friends with one, or are in love with one, this book's for you, too.

It'll help you learn more about how your empathic co-worker, or child, or friend, or beloved experiences the world. It'll help you to better communicate with and support your empath, which means less stress and conflict, and more harmony between you. Understanding your empath will making the world better for both of you.

We empaths are born with our psychic ability, but to make it a gift, as opposed to a burden, there are skills that we need to learn and information that we need to have. This book has the information that you need to help you learn to make the most of your gift.

We've got a lot of ground to cover together, so let's get started …

One
What is a Psychic Empath (and Am I One?...)

I don't know if everyone is psychic. I haven't met everyone yet; but, from my personal experience, it seems that most of the people in the world have some degree of psychic ability or other. From what I've seen, we seem to be hard-wired for psy as a species, and the variations seem primarily to be what kind of ability and how powerful.

There are quite a number of "flavors" of psychic ability. There are people who "see things" or have visions (clairvoyants). There are people who "hear things" (clairaudients). There are people who "just know things" (clairsentients). There are also people who perceive psychically through the senses of smell or taste. (These methods are less common.)

And then, there are people who feel things. This group breaks down into a number of subgroups, including people who get information from objects (psychometrists) and people who are sensitive to emotional vibrations (empaths). Informal studies indicate that empathy is the most frequently observed psychic skill in the general population. This may be because it's both immediately practical and also blends more easily with the non-psychic world. People with psychic empathy may be seen as "insightful", "compassionate", or "oversensitive", as opposed to more obviously psychic.

It's worth noting that, while most people have one strongest psychic sensory area, you can have more than one type of psychic perception. You can also strengthen more than one of these areas so you'll have a range of methods to use to tune in on the world around you. In this book, we'll focus on psychic empathy, but there are a lot of good books and classes out there on identifying and developing other psychic abilities.

While we're at it, let's take a moment to define the difference between psychological / social empathy and psychic empathy.

Social empathy is usually a feeling of compassion and kindness, triggered by seeing someone else in distress. Psychic empathy is access to information not available through the basic five senses, but instead by using your sixth sense to perceive emotional vibrations.

In social empathy, when someone is down or depressed, you feel sad for them.

In psychic empathy, when someone is depressed, you feel their depression as if it were your own (unless you have enough control of your gift to keep their emotional energy separate and distinct from your own.) You don't necessarily have to interact directly with them to feel their feelings. You may even pick up on these feelings if you are in the same area with someone without any direct contact.   As you can see, social empathy and psychic empathy are two very different things (though you may find that you have both types.)

As a psychic empath, you need techniques and skills so you can use your gift without being overwhelmed by the emotions of others.

The first step then, is to figure out whether you see the world through the eyes of psychic empathy.

Are You a Psychic Empath?

1) Do you cry easily?

2) Are you tuned in to or affected by people around you?

3) Do you have hunches or impressions about people that you can't explain?

4) Can you tell when someone is hurt or upset, even if there are no visible signs that this is the case?

5) When you trust your instincts, do you know who's trustworthy and who isn't?

6) Do you have an uneasy or sick feeling in the pit of your stomach when something's wrong, even if you don't know what it is yet? Do you "trust your gut"?

7) Can you tell when someone is being deceptive? Are you hard to fool if you listen to your inner wisdom?

8) Do you talk yourself out of feeling that something is wrong, only to find out that you were right all along? Does this happen repeatedly?

9) Are you frustrated because you don't "trust your gut" or listen to your instincts?

10) Have you been accused of being "oversensitive" or of overreacting?

11) Do you find that the only way that you can be happy is to make sure that everyone around you is happy?

12) Are you the peacemaker in your group?

13) When someone whispers angrily, does it feel like they're shouting?

14) Do your friends ask you what you think about people around them?

15) Are you uncomfortable in crowds?

16) Are you uncomfortable in the malls during the holiday season?

17) Are you uncomfortable at concerts, casinos or crowded sports events?

18) If you're with friends who are drinking, do you feel tipsy yourself, even if you haven't had any alcohol?

19) Does your good mood turn to a bad one if someone angry or

depressed walks into the room, even if they don't say a word to you?

20) Do the feelings of the people around you determine or affect your feelings?

21) Do you have a strong urge to "fix" things for people?

22) Do people bring their problems to you?

23) Do you make a living working closely with people? Or, contrariwise, do you make your living in a way that avoids as much human contact as possible?

24) Do you find that contact with people is often draining?

25) Do you need a certain amount of "alone time" as a regular part of your life to relax and rejuvenate?

26) When you're tired or sick, do you find that people are harder to tolerate?

27) Do people tell you that you're wrong or crazy; that your reactions are out of proportion to what is actually happening? Do you know that they're wrong, but let them convince you otherwise?

28) Do you tend to carry some extra weight in your stomach and abdomen?

29) Do you tend to frequently fold your arms across your chest or stomach when you're around people?

30) Do people tend to feel good when you're in a good mood? Contrariwise, if you're down, are you the ultimate "wet blanket"?

So, how'd you do? It's worth noting that many of these signs can happen for other reasons besides psychic empathy; however, the more of them that you have, the more likely it is that you are an empath.

Besides the signs and symptoms we've just looked at, there's another way to find out if you're a psychic empath. It comes from the art of palmistry (For more information on this, see my previous book "Adventures in Palmistry.")

In the palms of empaths, there's usually a mark called the

girdle of Venus. To find it, look at the bottom of your fingers in your dominant hand. The girdle of Venus is a ring running roughly from between the index and middle finger, to between the ring finger and pinkie.

See a complete semi-circle here? You're an empath. The darker that ring is, the stronger your gift. If the ring is present but incomplete or fragmented, you have the gift but are consciously or unconsciously trying to shut it down.

It's important to note that, as a person changes the direction of his life, his palms will change to reflect his new path. Because of this, a girdle of Venus can be incomplete when a person suppresses his gift, and later become whole if the person accepts and uses it.

Some of the indicators we've looked at apply to basic psychic empathy. Some apply to side effects of having the gift, but not the skills you need to control it.

Many of the quiz questions apply to more negative situations. Psychic empathy's not negative itself, but when you're looking for observable signs, the negative ones are often easier to spot as outside the normal range of human behavior, while positive aspects of empathy can look like doing normal things but doing them really, really well...

Up ahead, we'll be getting into these symptoms and challenges, and how to deal with them. First, though, we need to do some ground work in the language of energy, and the methods of metaphysics. Join me in the next chapter for a walk through the basics of energy.

Two
The Empath and Energy

When working in the field of metaphysics, whether in psychic abilities, alternative health, earth based magick, or unexplained phenomena, one thing you need to know about is energy. You need to know:

- How it behaves.
- How to move it.
- What affects it
- How you can control it.

Knowledge of energy is especially important for the psychic empath. Many empathic abilities and challenges revolve around emotional energy.

- Perceiving it;
- Reading it;
- Controlling how much you take in;
- Getting rid of excess, negative or "stuck" energy.

Let's start with how energy works. Every living thing is surrounded by a field of energy called the aura or auric field connecting with its physical form. This energetic field is made of layers, building outwards from your physical body.

Energy fields vary from being to being. The strength of your energy field reflects things such as your health, your personal energy, and non-corporeal factors, such as psychic abilities. Some are stronger, some are weaker; some larger, some smaller. Your energy field varies throughout your life, dependant on many factors, including the energy of the world around you.

It's even been found that future issues, like illness or injury, can be seen appearing in the outer layers of our energy field, gradually moving inwards until they arrive at the physical body at the time the health problem actually manifests. (It's also been noted that timely application of certain energetic techniques can interrupt this process, and head off the flu or the broken leg otherwise on its way.)

As we pass through the world, our energy fields overlap with those of others, and we can affect each other energetically, especially those of us with psychic abilities. The aura is open to such effects, unless a person develops energetic shields to prevent intrusion into the aura by the energy of others.

Your aura connects to your physical body via little vortexes of energy, known as chakras, located down the midline of your body and head, in your palms and the soles of your feet, and in other places throughout your body. Besides connecting your aura to your body, chakras are good for taking energy in and putting energy out, which is why touching something increases the strength of the energetic vibrations that you pick up from it.

This simple explanation of the energetic system is here to help explain how energetic techniques work for an empath. If you're interested in energy, there are other books that go into the aura and chakras in more detail.

When you're looking at energy, there are lots of types that are perfectly functional. There are also lots that can be problems. Let's take a quick look at these types of challenging energy and why you might want to avoid them.

Excessive energy – too much energy, whether positive or negative. When an empath encounters excess energy, he can feel overwhelmed or stressed. When an empath is carrying excessive energy (his own energy, or energy picked up from the world around him), it can be draining, exhausting, and cause health issues. Excessive energy can lead to mania, drunkenness, or hysteria.

Negative energy – includes depression, anxiety, anger, cynicism and other such emotions. When exposed to or carrying excess negative energy, an empath becomes negative himself. This can lead to health issues, stress, poor motivation and lack of resilience. It also means he is less able to keep his own energy shielded from energy around her. Negative energy can make you cynical, sick, sad, mad, depressed, or anxious.

"Stuck" energy – is old energy that you have been carrying around so long that you have forgotten that you are even carrying it. Old hurts and wounds. Long term beliefs. Grudges. Emotions that you can't seem to let go of. Some old luggage can be functional, but a lot of it is just dragging you down, and the fact that you've carried it for so long often makes it invisible to you. Carrying "stuck" energy can often be draining and debilitating.

There are some times when challenging emotions are appropriate, reasonable reactions to situations around you; when they're reactions to illness, stress, and/or insufficient sleep. These clear relatively easily, once the causes are gone.

To clear other challenging emotional vibrations, the psychic empath may need to use techniques learned later on in this book. Also, later in this book, you'll be looking at ways to evaluate the energy you're dealing with, to figure out what you need to do to resolve it.

There are a couple of other concepts about energy that the psychic empath needs in particular to know about.

The biggest challenge and most important skill for the empath is being able to manage and control the amount, quantity and type of emotional energy that he or she makes contact with. Too much emotional energy and the empath becomes overwhelmed, which can have serious negative effects on health, function and quality of life. Too little, and the empath loses not only the information that he can gain from his gift, but also meaning, social cues and a lot of other things that also make life good.

Throughout this book, I'll be using certain terms to describe the balance needed for successful empathy.

Control – To avoid being overwhelmed, an empath needs control over how much emotional energy he takes in. This might sound very stiff and rigid, but is actually more of a dynamic balance of taking in only as much energy as you can deal with at any particular moment.

Protection – This word can sound like the world is a hostile and dangerous place; but it actually refers to providing a barrier or separation between the empaths's energy and that of other people outside of him. This allows him to choose what energy he takes in and what will remain separate from him (as opposed to leaving him open and at the mercy of every energetic wind that blows...)

Just remember, to survive and thrive as an empath, it's all about learning to identify and manage energy.

Next, we'll be getting into basic metaphysical information that affects the empath.

Three
The Empath and the Science of Magick

In the last chapter, we laid the groundwork on energetic fields and working with energy. In this chapter, we're going to build on that foundation by looking at some of the basics of metaphysical workings.

Since this book is for and about the psychic empath, we'll be dealing with this from a psychic viewpoint, but there are topics and techniques that we'll be getting into where the easiest, clearest way to explain things is by using the language of metaphysics and magick.

Let's start with some definitions.

Magick – magick is the general term for affecting the world around you by esoteric or energetic means, whether it is by using spells, intention, chants, or by other such methods. It is spelled with a "k" on the end in order to distinguish it from stage magic/ illusions. Most cultures around the world have used some form of magick at some point in history to improve the world around them.

Intention - An intention is the goal you want your magick or energy work to accomplish. "Setting an intention" means using a method to shape energy to a purpose, whether writing your intention down, chanting it, holding it firmly in mind, etc...

Elements – Forces in nature believed to have identity, energy and power. Dependant on culture there are 4 (earth, air, fire, water) or 5 (the previous four plus metal).

As noted above, most cultures around the world have a history of some kind of magickal practice. One of the beliefs that is part of these practices is the concept of "the symbol is the thing." This is often referred to as the Law of Similarity.

For psychics, this means that, if we want to clear negative energy from ourselves, we already think of using water as a symbol for washing away things we don't want. This established association makes it easier for us to do clearing work using water on an energetic level (whether visualizing water or actually washing our hands).

If we want to build energetic shields to keep out unwanted energy, closing our eyes and picturing a castle's walls with defending soldiers can make our shields stronger.

If we want to cut off excess vibrations coming from someone with too much drama, picturing a sword or giant shears severing the connections between us and that person can give us relief.

We'll be using this simple idea often throughout this book to make doing techniques you need to master your empathy quicker and easier. I'll be giving you plenty of examples, but remember that it's perfectly o.k. to make up your own. If there's something that you're trying to do, and you already have experience with an object or tool that does something similar, you can use it (whether literally or by visualization) to accomplish your energetic task.

Just remember, in energy, the symbol is the thing.

Another key concept in the areas of magick, metaphysics and psychic work is that of intention, and of "setting an intention".

As noted above, an intention is what you want the energywork, or spell, or psychic perception to do. It's a metaphysical goal for the energy that you're working with.

You set an intention before you start working with energy. There are a number of ways to do this.

- You can formally declare it before you start working. (Ex.: "This visualization is to build stronger energetic shields.")
- You can focus your mind on it and hold this thought firmly while you are working energetically.
- You can write it down in a formal way that you have chosen for yourself.

- You can make an affirmation of it. (Ex.: "I am now releasing all negative energy", and repeat or chant this while you work.)
- Or, you can make up your own way of setting your intention for the energywork that you are doing.

The work itself generates energy to shift the nature of reality ever so slightly. The intention serves as the lens on a laser, to focus all of that energy towards the task it was meant to do.

I've been talking about energywork. There are lots of different ways to work with energy. You can:

- Meditate;
- Visualize;
- Affirm;
- Chant:
- Drum or make other noises;
- Write things down;
- Follow a formula, otherwise known as a spell;
- Use physical activity to move energy, such as dance;

And that's just a few examples.

We'll be using a number of these methods of working with energy as we learn different skills throughout this book. Just keep in mind, there is no "one-size-fits-all".

Some people are meditators, and others are dancers, or drummers, or casters of spells. If one type of energywork doesn't work as well for you, it's perfectly fine to translate that method into a different form of energywork - one that is a better fit for your particular needs.

One final metaphysical point – that of gratitude.

Most metaphysical practices find that, if one is appreciative of and grateful for the good things you already have in your life, it becomes much easier to attract or manifest more good things.

And contrariwise, if you're focused on the negative things in your life, you tend to attract more of those.

From a psychic empath's standpoint then, this has two equally important aspects.

First, internal gratitude will help you. Even if you are currently feeling overwhelmed because you have the gift but not the techniques you need to control it yet, you're going to find it far easier to learn those skills and get that control if you focus on anything positive in your life. So, it's good to count your blessings.

Secondly, external gratitude can also help you. In many various exercises throughout this book, we will be utilizing the four elements, earth, air, fire and water, (amongst many other things) to help clear, release, and transform excess, negative or "stuck" energy.

In many cultures, these elements are considered to be sentient beings of power.

Do you have to believe this to work with the four elements for grounding out unwanted energy? Not necessarily, but it's good to know that this is one way of seeing the elements.

Keep in mind that you're getting help in managing the energy around you from these elements. At that point, it's appropriate to express gratitude for that help.

So when you finish an exercise where you receive help from an element, it's good to say "thanks".

Psychic work and magickal work are not the same thing, but they do have areas of overlap that can be useful to people on either end of the spectrum. Both sides have healers. Both sides perceive energy. Both sides do readings, using techniques or tools. And it behooves us to learn from our energetic neighbors down the way what we can of the wisdom they have that might serve our own needs.

You don't need to follow Wicca or become a shaman to find the commonalities between the psychic and metaphysical communities. The more that you learn, the more you know about what best serves your own unique personal needs.

In the next chapter, we'll be talking more about what it means to be a psychic empath.

Four
The Ups and Downs of Psychic Empathy

Empathy can be a wonderful gift... or a tremendous burden. It all depends on how you work with it.

When a person is born with empathy, she's gifted psychically, but overly open and vulnerable to emotional energy around her. Without control of energetic input she receives, she may have problems interacting with people or functioning in normal situations, due to all of the pressure on her from emotions she's exposed to. This pressure can be exhausting and draining to an empath, and can affect her health in body, mind and spirit.

.   While being an empath isn't unhealthy in itself, it can be very stressful when the emotions of everyone that you meet are slam dancing in your energy field without your permission. Ongoing stress can depress your immune system, raise your blood pressure, give you anxiety and panic attacks; shoot your blood sugar up and down, and have a number of other negative effects on your overall health. To stay healthy, you need to manage stress. Controlling energetic input is one thing that an empath needs to learn to do this, and stay healthy. When you have no control of your empathy, it can have a negative effect on almost every area of your life.

On the other hand, the functional empath who has learned the skills she needs to control her gift (as opposed to let her gift control her) is able to use that gift for better information, making better connections between people, and to help herself and the people around her. She can read the information her empathy brings to her, without experiencing the emotions of others as if they were her own. She is able to maintain the positive energy she needs to make good use of her gift.

Let's take a more specific look at the positives and the negatives of psychic empathy.

On the plus side, it can give you true insight into the people around you.

What's that good for?

Well, amongst other things....

- understanding people you meet in your daily life;
- nurturing people you care about;
- overcoming misunderstandings;
- knowing when people are upset or in trouble;
- helping you make wiser, more informed choices;
- knowing who can be trusted and who can't;
- protecting your own personal safety and that of people around you;
- helping folks really understand each other and reach common ground together;
- making your little corner of the cosmos a kinder, better place to be;

And a lot of other fun and useful applications for better living. Sounds good, right?

On the flip side of the coin, if you're an empath who hasn't yet gotten control of your gift:

- You can be overwhelmed by the feelings of people around you.
- You may experience other people's feelings in your own body as if they were your own feelings. An encounter with someone who is cranky (or depressed or euphoric...) can make you feel cranky, depressed, or euphoric too, even if you were having a great day before that person came along.
- Because this can happen without a word spoken between you and the person with the emotion, you may find yourself "having mood swings" that are actually someone else's emotions you've picked up unknowingly. This can masquerade as manic depression or other such conditions, and make you feel more than a little crazy.
- Sometimes people may see you as "over-sensitive", "over-reacting", wrong, or even crazy, because you react

to emotional energy that they don't perceive.

- The erratic emotional input that you're living with, mixed with negative input from people who don't experience things empathically, can leave you doubting yourself, your judgment and even your sanity; even though what you're feeling is accurate.

- You may know that something is "off", "wrong" or otherwise out of whack, but let non-psychic people around you convince you that you're overreacting or over sensitive. Then, when it turns out that you were right all along, you can feel frustrated, guilty or angry with yourself. This is a brilliant recipe for poor self esteem. (In extreme cases, you can even find yourself going the self-loathing route, where you beat yourself up for not listening to yourself, doing additional damage in the process.)

Other possible symptoms of the "less-than-ideal" side of empathy:

- Mild to severe discomfort with crowds, especially ones of depressed, angry, intense or cranky people (Ex: sports matches, political rallies, casinos, the malls at Christmas).

- Frustration with people who say they're feeling one thing when they're actually feeling another (even if they're doing it in a mistaken attempt to be kind.)

- Finding confrontation harder than most people do (because people are yelling with their emotions as well as their mouths.)

- Increased stress, which can mess with your digestion; increase anxiety and panic; trash your immune system (leaving you vulnerable to whatever's "going around"); increase your blood pressure, (raising the chances of cardiovascular issues); and lead to a host of other very special health issues.

- A need to make people around you happy or to "fix" them, because having happy, content people around you is the only way you can be happy yourself.

I've been there, done that, bought the T-shirt. For years, my theme song was "I want to be happy, but I can't be happy 'til I make you happy, too (drat!)"It took me quite awhile to finally get a handle on how to make empathy truly a gift to me and the planet.

The way to deal with a majority of the negative aspects of empathy is to learn the skills that give you control of your gift. That's what this book is about.

It's worth noting that it's not simply negative energy that's a problem for empaths.

An excess of negative emotional energy can cause you to pick up negative emotions yourself. It can make you angry, frustrated, or depressed. Too much negative energy can be exhausting and draining. It can mess with your immune system, boost your blood pressure, increase your stress levels, and leave you open to all manner of health problems in body, mind and spirit.

On the other hand, too much *positive* energy, can make you giddy or manic, and impair your judgment. It can also be exhausting or draining, and mess with your health in many of the same ways that an excess of negative energy can. (The one major plus is that you'll probably feel better while it goes to work on you…)

If you must choose between the two types of energy, positive energy is much healthier and easier to deal with than negative energy. You need to remember, though, that too much of either can be rough on you.

On top of the question of positive and negative energy, you also need to keep in mind that the amount of any kind of energy you can handle is affected by what's going on in your life at the time.

- Things going smoothly? You can probably handle increased energy.
- Got a cold? You're more easily thrown off center.
- Good things happening? More energy? No problem!
- Things falling apart? Time to withdraw....

The key to thriving as a psychic empath is balance and control. Being able to determine how much outside energy you can deal with and choose to accept into your life at any particular moment.

Most empaths get helpful information from emotional energy, but that's not always true. I've met people who perceive emotional energy, but can't identify the emotions received. Folks like this often have problems identifying and responding to emotions in non-psychic, social situations as well. Given the increase in conditions like autism or Aspergers (with problems with identifying emotional cues), it's possible this type of empath has other challenges blocking her ability to "read" emotions.

This can be a problem. You have the disadvantages of being open / vulnerable to emotions, without the help empathic awareness can bring you.

Fortunately, there are ways around this. The non-psychic person with problems reading emotional cues can often train to learn to recognize them. An empath with problems "reading" emotional energy can also learn the feel of different energies, as well as techniques for shielding and controlling his energetic intake. It can take a bit more work, but it's worth it.

In addition to all of this, all empaths are receptive empaths. This means taking in and being aware of the emotional vibrations of people around them.

Some empaths are also projective empaths. Their emotional vibrations tend to affect the people around them. (They can't control the emotions that folks around them feel, but they can influence them, whether consciously or unconsciously).

This can be a good thing or a bad thing...

A projective empath can be the life of the party, or the ultimate wet blanket. This variety of empath, on top of everything else we've listed above, needs to gain control of how much and what kind of emotional vibrations she's sharing with the world around her.

Some people are threatened or overwhelmed by having a psychic gift such as empathy. They wonder if they really have to possess a psychic gift they never asked for and do not particularly want. They want to shut it down.

I've had had people ask me how to do this. I've also seen people try to do this on their own.

I've seen people intentionally or unintentionally try to shut their gift down completely. I've seen people consciously or unconsciously build shields so thick that they completely block out all normal levels of energetic emotional input. I've seen people go into denial, saying that psychic abilities are not for real, that only "special people" have such abilities, or that they're imagining impressions their empathy is giving them. I've seen people do a lot of different things in order to block or negate their innate psychic empathy.

Is this a good idea or not?

Well, there are certain situations under which it may be wisest to minimize or shut down your gift temporarily:

- If you're living in an abusive situation, you may wish to cut down all sensitivity (which makes you more vulnerable to damage), except for what's needed to watch out for danger. This is only temporary until you can escape from that situation.

- If you are living or working in a situation where one or more people is severely ill or seriously depressed, you might want to adjust your sensitivity so you can be kind, compassionate and caring, but not suffer due to the circumstances.
- If you were in a war zone or hazardous part of the world, you might want to adjust your sensitivity so you get an advance heads up of any dangerous activity in the offing, without taking in and feeling the emotions of people who really don't like you.

There are certainly a number of really good reasons why you might need to restrain or shut down an empathic gift, but these would all be part time or temporary adjustments.

Most of the methods listed above would make adequate make-shift or band-aid types of remedies. They work temporarily, but as long term solutions, they leave a lot to be desired. Problems with such "solutions" include:

- People with this kind of solution may find that they work out fine for a short time or for ordinary daily levels of energy. Eventually, though, there always comes a time when the level of emotional energy around them increases to the point where the make-shift solution gives way. At that point, unexpected emergency levels of energy hit the empath right in the face. Having approached his gift by denying it, the empath in this situation has no resources or skills to fall back on, and usually gets smacked pretty hard by the energetic informational overflow.
- People who shut down their empathy may find that they become less aware of basic human social cues. This can

cause problems in a number of ways.

- People who turn off their empathy can find themselves feeling "blah", morose, or even depressed. There can be a feeling of something missing in life.
- People can talk themselves out of information their gift is giving them. (Ex:"That's silly. How could I possibly know that?" or "I'm just being paranoid") They can get very angry when they find that the thing that they talked themselves out of was true all along. They can even develop poor self esteem or self loathing from working so hard to not listen to what they are trying to tell themselves.
- People who work hard to talk themselves out of what their empathy is telling them may find themselves getting jumpy, anxious or even paranoid. They tell themselves that all of this information doesn't really exist, but they can still perceive it and react to every little alert before they talk themselves out of it. The constant level of adrenalin jump can play hob with their ability to stay calm and centered.
- People who shut down their gift long term often find themselves feeling isolated or lonely.

Limiting or shutting your gift down long term can have the kind of side effects that you may not want to experience personally. If you want good control over the gift of psychic empathy, the best way to get it is to acknowledge and understand your gift, and work with it for what it is.

The best way to adapt your level of sensitivity to your individual personal needs or situations is to learn how to have, use and adapt your own personal energetic shields. Energetic shields are a way of letting you perceive energy, while keeping it from going into your body and affecting you directly. Once you have shields, there are other things you can do to control the type and amount of emotional energetic input you have to deal with, but shields are where we start.

So, what do we need to do in order to tap into the good stuff that goes with psychic empathy while letting the "less-than-ideal" stuff go? The answer lies in gaining new skills - the skills that you need to be able to perceive the emotions of others without taking those emotions into yourself and experiencing them as your own. In my experience, empaths are born with their empathy but only get the skills they need to manage it successfully if they learn and develop them for themselves.

What do you need to learn? You need to learn:

- How to keep your emotional energy and that of other people separate.
- How to limit or cut off a flow of emotional energy coming from outside of you.
- How to have an energetic "set point" (a standard positive level of personal emotional energy that is your usual condition) and how to keep your energy at this level, in order to offset the effect of the other people's energy on you.
- How to perceive the information that emotional energy has to give you without taking other people's emotions into yourself or experiencing them as your own.
- How to protect yourself from negative energy, whether it's negative energy that's part of everyday life, or the more powerful, intrusive energy linked with stressful people, environments or situations.
- How to ground out or release negative energy you don't need, whether you have picked it up from other people or

generated it for yourself.

- How to control the emotional energy that you project outwards to the world around you.

That sounds like an awful lot of things to do, right? Well, it is ... and it isn't.

Right now, you're probably working pretty hard just to stay afloat and cope with the demands put on you by energetic emotional input you don't have any control over. This can be exhausting, and learning these skills will lift that burden from you. Every single one of these skills that you learn will make your life easier, and that offsets the effort you need to put in to learn the skill in the first place.

Related to that, some people wonder if it's hard work to keep shields and other techniques up and running on an ongoing basis.

I find it may take some effort at first. You're not used to doing these techniques. As you practice them, they'll become unconscious habits, until they're so automatic that they're not any effort at all.

Once you've gotten used to them, you'll find yourself wondering how you got along without them.

We've got simple ways to learn these skills in this book for you. And, since different people have different approaches to life, we've got a lot of different techniques for each area of skill - enough techniques that you'll be able to pick and chose the ones that best meet your own specific needs.

Once you've gained the skills you need to learn so that

you have good control of your empathy, you'll be ready to enjoy your gift and put your empathy at the service of yourself and the world around you.

Sounds like a pretty good trade off to me...

But before we get into skills, we first need to go over ethical behavior for psychics. You need to learn the right way to use your skills with respect for yourself and all people, psychic or not.

And that's what we'll be doing in the next chapter

Five
A Question of Ethics; and Manners for Psychics

Let's talk about psychic ability and ethics.

As you make your way through this book, you'll be learning how to develop your psychic skills – skills that will give you better control of your empathic gift, and teach you how to use it for your benefit, and for the benefit of the world around you.

As a functional psychic, you have the advantage of access to information that most people do not have. That's the good news. The not – so – good news is that there's some of this information that's ethical for you to have and use – and some of it that's not....

As a psychic empath, it's ethical for you to read the surface energy of a person. That's energy that comes out to meet you. It's not ethical, in most cases, to energetically probe more deeply into another person's energy field, unless invited to do so by that person. (For instance, if someone invites you to "read" them psychically.)

When you were growing up, did your mom ever tell you not to pry into other peoples' business? Mine did. And it's kind of like that...

Let me give you another example of what I'm talking about. In physical space, it's o.k. to look at the smile or the frown on a person's face and get information about their mood from that. It's o.k. to read their body language and learn from that as well. It's not o.k. to go to their house at night without permission, and peek in their windows to see what you can see.

For any type of psychic, but especially for empaths, there is some energetic information that floats on the surface of a person's energy field, like a cheerful smile or a cranky frown on a person's face. Just as you can ethically read the emotion on that face, it's o.k. to get information from that surface energy.

There is also some emotional information that is so doggoned energetically loud that you could not screen it out unless you could stuff your metaphysical fingers into your esoteric ears. Those "loud" emotional vibrations are also energy that you are entitled to tap into for your own personal information or use.

Those are both public kinds of energy - energy right out there in the open for all to see who have the ability. As public emotional energy, you have as much of a right to access it as you do to access any other public things.

On the other hand, there is some emotional energy that is held deep, personal and private. That energy is hands off for the empathic psychic, unless, for some reason, the person in question gives you permission to look deeper. Indeed, unless you have a serious reason to go there, you're probably going to be much happier if you let those private things stay private, and keep your psychic senses out of their psyche.

(Many people's deepest feelings have more than a bit in common with the containers on the back shelf of the average refrigerator. A person may be absolutely delightful, but still not necessarily expect anyone to drop by and take a peek at his feelings, so the "personal" energetic areas may not have been tidied up for company....)

At times, due to being overwhelmed or stressed, or experiencing a triggering event (the proverbial last straw), some people's deep, private emotional energy may burst through from out of the depths of their being up to the surface of their energy field. Sometimes, it can even reach out beyond the person's energetic field, creating an overall tangible field of powerful emotions around them. This tends to be severe emotion, and is often very negative or painful, both for the person who owns it originally, and for the hapless empath who just happens to be passing by when the emotion peaks (There she blows, captain!...)

Private energy is private; but when private energy bursts loose, you cannot help but experience it, even if it is supposed to be secret, hidden and off limits to you and others. It is not unethical to perceive this energy when you get sideswiped by it, although you may end up knowing far more than you really wanted to know about the situation.

When overwhelming private emotional energy erupts, this

is a time when it's good for you to break out your handy little toolbox of energetic tricks that you'll learn in this book. Using these techniques can help keep your energy separate from that of other people, and protect you from receiving that overwhelming energy into yourself. Do the best you can to control the flow of energy, and how much comes into your own energy field. If you have that control, you can keep your head, and do something productive in the situation at hand, rather than be totally swamped by the explosive emotional energy.

Public emotional energy is public, and you have every right to look at it and use what you learn from it. Private emotional energy is private, and you shouldn't really be delving into it, unless invited to do so, or unless this private energy is thrust upon you.

So keep in mind that, while you'll have the ability to learn about people from their emotional energy, you won't always have the right to do so.

I just said that private emotional energy is private. That you shouldn't probe deeply into the emotions of others, unless that energy's thrust on you, or unless you are given permission.

That being said, there are certain exceptions to this rule. And most of these situations involve your safety and the safety of people that you care for...

First and foremost, we're talking about your physical safety and that of those you love; but also safety in financial arrangements, legal agreements, professional relationships, and other situations where dishonesty, greed or violence could do you harm.

In such a situation, your first warning of a problem can be a vague feeling of unease, the classic "butterflies in the stomach". (Remember, those "butterflies" are fluttering around the psychic center for empathic reception...)

First, do a quick scan of the environment around you, looking for obvious risk factors. This is a rapid safety check, to determine whether your current position is safe enough for you to stop and focus on your empathic input without making yourself more vulnerable to harm.

- Is the situation physically safe? Is there the potential present for a person, item or situation to physically harm you? (Ex: are you walking through a potentially dangerous area alone in the dark?)
- Are you about to make a commitment, sign a document, or otherwise lock yourself into a situation where you could experience long term harm, if someone is not being honest with you? (Ex: are you about to sign an agreement to buy a home, but have not yet had the building inspected?)
- Are you about to put yourself in a position where you will be especially vulnerable to a person, especially one that you do not know well? (Ex: are you about to accept a ride home with a person that you've just met?)

Or other such circumstances of this sort...

If you feel like something's wrong, and your situation is potentially unsafe in any way, such as the above ones, your first step is to withdraw from the immediate situation to a safer location, where you can access your empathic talent without being at immediate risk.

Make an excuse not to sign at this time. Withdraw to a public space with more people. Say thank you, but you'll get a ride home with someone else.

Many times, people will have these "butterflies" and talk themselves out of them.

- "Oh, that's just silly!"
- "He's a perfectly nice man..."

- "Who do you think you are to have a special gift like that?"
- "How could I possibly know something like that?"

How indeed? But when you've become aware of your empathic gift, one of the more self destructive things you can do is to rationalize it away when it is seriously trying to warn you about something.

You may sometimes be kidding yourself. Everyone does at one point or another. Once you acknowledge your gift, however, it will do its best to keep you safe and happy. Many times, rationalizing these warnings away involves putting yourself down in order to discredit the message you are getting. This means that you get the rare treat of feeling bad at least three times-

- Once when you rank on yourself for "telling yourself stories",
- Once when the bad thing happens that your empathetic gift was trying to warn you about,
- And once more when you realize that you were right all along, but that you talked yourself out of it.

And who really needs that?

You don't always need to burn your bridges, cancel your options, run screaming into the night whenever your empathy sets off the warning bells. Many times, it's just an alert to slow down and pay attention, because something is not right. To "Stop, Look. And Listen.", as they used to say about crossing the street when I was a child.

Sometimes you'll find that those "butterflies" are only ordinary things, like stage fright, shyness or the side effects of moving outside of your comfort zone, But many times, they are the first warnings that a psychic empath has that something is not right, and you will rarely do yourself wrong by stopping what you're doing, withdrawing to a position of greater safety, and then pausing to tap more deeply into your empathic senses...

If you are in a relatively safe situation at the moment, stop then and look inwards. Energetically "reach out" with your spirit, just as if you were reaching out with your arm, and see what information you can gather. Listen to your body, and what it has to tell you. Listen to your inner wisdom, and what it has to say. Trust your gut. Closing your eyes and breathing deeply can sometimes help you get in better contact with your empathy, and help you to reach deeper into the energy you are reading.

Questions you should be asking yourself include:

- What is your body telling you?
- What is your "gut instinct"?
- Do you feel cautious? Uneasy? Scared?
- What "feels wrong" or "off" to you?

With practice and time, the messages you need to get in such circumstances will become much clearer to you. Amongst other things, you'll learn the difference between things such as stage fright, and actual warnings of danger.

Sometimes, the message may be to wait and gather more information. Sometimes it's that what you're thinking about is not as sound as you thought it was. Sometimes it's that you need to leave an area. And sometimes it's that the person you're facing does not have your best interests at heart (and the degree of that may vary.)

When the situation is unsafe, it's certainly alright to reach beyond the surface emotion of others to gather information to ensure your own safety and that of those you care for. This is only ethical to gain enough information to remain safe from harm. You should take only what you need to keep yourself safe, and no more than that.

Remember that, other than this kind of situation regarding safety, it's still not ethical to delve into the emotional energy that runs deeper than the energetic surface layers of a person. A deeper empathic probe should be the exception, and not the rule.

This technique will be more effective for you once you've learned some of the ways to protect your emotional energy from the energy of others, but even before you start learning these techniques, you're in a good position to start listening to your intuition for your own safety, as well as learning the ethics of empathy.

You now have a basic grounding in ethics – in the ethical path of the psychic. But ethics alone are not enough to give you control of your psychic empathy.

You need more than knowledge – you need skills. The skills to have better control of your gift

And the first and the foremost skill that you, as a psychic empath, needs is the knowledge of how to form and utilize good energetic shields, how to adapt them to meet your specific individual needs for different situations, and the skill to use them effectively

How lucky that we have that information for you.

So follow me now to the next chapter where we'll talk about different types of energetic shields, and how you can make them your own…

Six
Energetic Shields – an Empath's Best Friend

One of the most important things that a psychic empath can have is good energetic shields. So what are they, anyway?

Shields are a field of protective metaphysical energy that surrounds you. They keep your energy safe inside of the shields; and other folks' energy safe outside of them. They separate other people's energy from yours, but keep it perceptible to you, so you can still feel it and know what the energy is trying to tell you. (I like to think of it as the difference between "mine and thine" in emotional vibrations.) Picture shields as being like a science fiction-type force field designed specifically for emotional energy. A good set of energetic shields will let you perceive what's going on around you on an emotional level, without leaving you beaten up by every emotional wavelength that comes along.

For years, my shields were as full of holes as a macramé pot-holder. I was at the mercy of every emotional wind that blew. Developing decent shields made my life much better and put me in touch with the positive side of empathy.

And it can do the same for you.

How do you get good energetic shields? You can't just go to the local department store and pick them up in the "energetic shields" department...

That's why this chapter is here. We're going to teach you a number of ways to develop and work with shields, starting with a simple but effective way to create your own.

<u>Building Basic Energetic Shields</u>

Whenever you have a moment (or two or three or ten...), close your eyes and picture yourself surrounded by light. Light to the left of you and to the right; light in front of you and in back of you; light over your head and under your feet; so that you are surrounded completely on all sides by light.

What color of light? Tradition holds that it should be

white as that is the highest, purest, and best color, and also because it contains all of the other colors within it.

I say that you should choose whatever color makes you feel safest, calmest, and best with yourself.

- Do you like green? Great!
- Want pink? Right on!
- If you want plaid, I'm for it!

You can also have more than one color if you like. My own shields tend to be white with a golden edge. As you visualize this light, it's good to set an intention to define what your shields will do for you. As noted in chapter three, an intention is just a thought that sets a concrete goal for what you want the shield to do.

- Intend that you'll be completely protected from any energy that might harm you in body, mind or spirit;
- Intend that the only energy that touches you directly is energy you have consciously chosen to allow;
- Intend that you will be aware of energy around you, but that it can't effect you directly or indirectly;
- Intend that your shields are always protecting you unless you consciously chose to let them down;

You get the idea.

What would you like your shields to do?

One really good option is setting your intention that your shields only let emotional energy actually touch you if you consciously choose to let it do so. Intend that any emotional energy that comes flying across the room at you will stop at the outside edge of your shields. (I tend to think of it as being like a bug on a windshield...) That you'll be able to perceive what that energy has to tell you without taking it into yourself, experiencing it as your own feelings and becoming overwhelmed.

If you use this shield intention or another of your choice, you'll find that your shields will become strong but flexible over time, able to give you the coverage you need in any situation, without cutting you off from the benefits of psychic empathy.

Pretty cool, that. And all for the cost of a little focused daydreaming…

By holding your intention for your shields firmly in mind while you visualize them, you program the energy of the shields with the purpose(s) you have set for them.

In time, as you visualize your shields of light around you, you'll find that you feel more protected; and more able to cope with the energy that surrounds you. You'll be less vulnerable to that emotional energy. You'll be able to read the energy without having those emotions enter your body and feel like they are your own.

I've had some people ask me if it's hard work or wearing on a person to keep energetic shields up all of the time as a default setting for life. If you build them up gradually, using the "egg of light" visualization above or something like it, you'll find it becomes an unconscious habit with practice, and, effortless for all intents and purposes as you get used to it. Furthermore, you may find that you actually have *more* energy, not less, once you start doing this regularly, because you're not constantly dealing with the stress of experiencing everyone's emotional energy directly.

This exercise builds basic general energetic shields that are effective for most empaths. Because every person is an individual, you may find that, once you've got your shields up, they may do the job, but be not quite a perfect fit for you. (After all, one size fits all is usually a pretty fairy tale).

You may find that you want to vary the strength of your shields for different settings or situations, such as home and work, or small groups versus big crowds. You may want to be able to adjust your shields so that you have increased sensitivity for situations like signing contracts or walking home after dark. You may want to be able to increase the thickness of your shields for the obligatory visits to an obnoxious relation. You may want to tune your shields so that they permit more energetic input from people that you trust, and limit input from people that you don't know.

Once you've been working for awhile with basic visualization for building energetic shields, you'll probably find that you're getting better control over how emotional energy around you affects you. You have more ability to chose - chose what energy you let in and what you chose to keep outside of you.

What if your basic shields aren't always enough?

In every person's life, there are times that particularly test us- even if you have great shields:

- In the face of open bigotry;
- In the malls before Christmastime;
- When the one you love is really, really, **really** ticked at you;

We all face times when the stakes are high, the energy is flowing double-time (…or triple-time, or a hundred-fold…), and our shields feel like we've built them out of pure Swiss cheese (nice, but full of holes…)

What's a poor empath to do?

When your basic shields are functioning fairly well, you can begin to tweak your visualizations and/or your intent in order to fine-tune your shields to best meet your unique personal needs. That's what we're going to do next.

This is the point where you give your shields an upgrade…

Energetic Shields Upgrade

Start with your basic shields. Set your intention that the basic shields you've built will be on at all times, unless you consciously chose to take them down. Add a further intention that, at times that are energetically challenging, you can consciously choose to increase those shields according to your personal needs.

What do I mean by "increase"? Well, you can make your shields:

- Stronger;
- Thicker;
- More resilient (so that any negative or unwanted energy bounces off of them and far away from you. Think "I'm rubber and you're glue...");
- More powerful;
- More energetic (up the amperage);
- More adhesive (so that negative energy gets stuck at the edge of your shields and is unable to reach you);
- Any combination of the above;
- Or any other concept that works for you...

Choose the variation of shield you would like for a more challenging situation, or create your own image that would work for you when things get rougher.

Picture your standard shields first, holding the intention that this is the level that is always running, unless you consciously chose to let it down.

Then visualize the upgrade version. Hold the intention in mind, heart and soul that, if things get more challenging, your shields will upgrade automatically to this level, and stay here until you consciously choose to return to your basic setting. You can also add an intention that you can consciously choose to upgrade them in situations that you find uncomfortable, but that are not bad enough yet to automatically trigger the upgrade state. (Like having a thermostat on your shields that includes both automatic programming and a manual override).

When you visualize the upgrade of your energetic shields, it may help to use an image that goes with the function you've chosen for that upgrade (i.e. picture a thicker shield for stronger, a brighter shield for increased energy, and so forth). The different image will both help the upgrade become functional faster, and also give you a mental handle to use to switch manually to the upgrade, if you need to.

Just as with basic shield construction, you'll find over time that you're not only more insulated from casual emotional wavelengths around you, but also that your shields automatically adjust when things get more stressful in order to take the increased strain.

In extra tough times, I like to mentally "flare" the energy in my shields, picturing an increased burst of color and vibration. I then push that extra energy outwards with my mind. It makes my shields feel stronger and more powerful, and gives me more control over what outside energy I choose to accept. It also tends to push negative energy further away from me, where most of us prefer negative energy to be. This makes it easier for me to find my center again and better deal with what is happening around me at any moment

Once you've got the basic and the upgrade shields in place, it's good to make a routine of practicing a "shields up!" response, getting it in place as a familiar option at a time while things are relatively calm in your life. Doing this means that, when you need them, you'll have built the upgraded shields, the automatic default setting, and the habit of consciously using them when you chose to.

And you'll be ready for whatever Life brings you...

Speaking of heavier shields, sometimes you'll find someone you can't feel at all- someone who energetically feels like "dead space". This is usually someone who, consciously or unconsciously, has developed such extremely thick shields that no emotional energy leaks through at all.

Now, I've heard that some people say that shields are a bad idea if you're psychic. That you don't know what wonderful thing you may be shutting out with your shields.

This is why I tend to build energetic shields that are impenetrable, but translucent. I want a shield that lets me perceive what is happening, without experiencing it directly or by surprise- because there are plenty of less than pleasant "surprises" drifting around out there.

Due to my own experience, I personally believe that an empath needs shields, if only to keep from being mugged at random by the bad mood of the guy in the next cubicle. I believe an empath needs the chance to choose consciously what energy he lets into his own energy field and body, and which he keeps out. (Kind of like some of those swankier dance clubs with the long lines, bouncers and the velvet rope…)

It's your energy field. You should have the right to choose whose energy you want to play host to, and whose energy you do not. Shields let you do that…

If you have good shields and good control of those shields, you'll have a standard setting for everyday life, one that keeps general energy outside of you and gives you a heads up to observe what is happening, so you can choose whether you want to let it in.

You'll have a stronger setting for more challenging situations, like controversial weddings, white sales and being on reality shows.

And you'll have the option of choosing to lessen or drop your shields by your conscious choice in any situation when you choose to share the emotional energy of others more closely.

Include the intention to know what is happening while being protected from overwhelming energy around you. This gives you the freedom to choose what energy you take into yourself, rather than everything that comes by or that is thrust at you willy-nilly.

Sometimes, you're going to want to be able to lower your shields to a low level, or even possibly to temporarily turn them off altogether.

When might you want to do this?

- When playing with your happy, silly, giggly child;
- When you're having a romantic time with someone you trust;

- When you're with even-tempered friends who are drinking, and who stay happy when drinking;
- When you're in a safe situation and it's important to more fully receive and understand the subtle emotional nuances of people that you're working with, negotiating with or trying to reach an agreement with;
- When you're spending time doing something fun, like watching fireworks, with positive people;
- When you're on stage doing a performing art, such as singing or acting, and you want to add projected emotion to the ways that you reach your audience;
- When you want to make a strong non-verbal connection with someone, and that person is unlikely to be experiencing significant negative energy that they might share with you;
- When you need to listen as deeply as possible; and listen with your spirit, as well as your ears;

There are quite a number of times when you might want heightened sensitivity as opposed to more powerful shielding. At that point, you'll need the option to choose consciously to dial down or even turn off your shields. You'll also want the added condition that, if things should suddenly get more lively, your shields automatically return to the standard setting, or even snap up to the upgrade level, if it seems necessary for the situation at hand.

And so, we offer you light level shields …

Light Level Shields

Start with your visualization of your basic shields. Hold them firmly in your mind until you see them clearly, without strain. By this point, having had so much practice with this exercise, you'll probably find this easy.

Once you have your basic shields clearly in your mind, then picture them becoming lighter or turning down or off by your choice.

There are a number of ways that you can do this.

- You can picture your shields becoming more muted, and less bright or shiny.
- You can picture your shields becoming thinner or more diffuse.
- You can picture a volume knob and your hand dialing the volume of your shields down.
- You can picture a colorful gauge or dial that indicates the intensity of your shields; and see the needle that shows the power level of your shields going down as you concentrate on it.
- You can picture a light switch and see yourself turning it off. (A dimmer switch is another option.)
- Or, you can use an image of your personal choice.

The key is finding the image that works best for you, and using it to adjust the intensity of your shields.

As you visualize, set the intention that your shields remain at standard level, unless you consciously choose to upgrade them, decrease them, or turn them off altogether.

Also set the intention that, if you have chosen to turn your shields down or off, and your situation becomes more energetically challenging, your shields will return automatically to the standard level, or move to the upgrade level if the situation requires it.

As you practice these adjustments to your shields, take a moment at each different level and pay attention to how much energy you feel reaching you at that level of shield intensity. Knowing how much energetic coverage you have at each level makes it easier to consciously choose the best level of shield to use at any time.

Just as while creating basic and upgrade shields, you'll find that, with practice, it becomes easier for your shields to automatically adapt to whatever level of intensity you need at any moment. The proper level is important, in order to keep you aware of what's going on around you, but protected from overwhelming energetic input as well. You'll find that, when things get tough, your shields automatically will adjust to take the increased strain.

And that is where you want to be...

Let's summarize at this point. If you've done all of the exercises for energetic shields, you should have:

- Standard level energetic shields, which:
    - Are automatically active whenever you don't choose something else;
    - Provide enough coverage to keep you from being overwhelmed by the energy of a standard day;
    - Still permit you to be aware of what is going on around you energetically while providing energetic protection;
- Upgrade level energetic shields, which:
    - Are coverage for more intense situations;
    - Provide increased protection, at the expense of decreased energetic informational input;
    - Can be set to activate automatically, in the event of situations of rapidly increasing energetic intensity;
    - Can be consciously chosen in a situation that is increasingly uncomfortable, but not yet escalated to the point where your shields automatically upgrade;
- Decreased or light level energetic shields, which:
    - Are appropriate to times when emotional energy around you is light or consistently safe, pleasant or supportive;
    - Are activated through conscious choice;
    - Provide increased sensitivity and awareness, at the expense of decreased protection;

- If you have light shields on, and things become more volatile, the shields should automatically return to standard levels, or even jump to the upgrade level, if the situation warrants this;

- And a "shields off" setting, which:
  - Is appropriate primarily for when you are in a very safe situation, or when you are alone;
  - Provides a high degree of sensitivity, at the expense of any protection;
  - Has most of the other characteristics of the decreased or light shield setting;

This is assuming that you have built your shields according to the original exercises as written. You may not have – and, if so, that's fine with me. Since everyone is a unique individual, with their own specific needs, it's most important to build the shields that **you** need, as opposed to hew to the letter of the exercise.

If you work in a chaotic institution, you may need stronger shields as your default setting. If your environment is more positive, you may not need as much shielding. And if your circumstances change quickly and often, your shields may have to do the same.

The bottom line is you need to have shields that work for you, and work in the situations you are in.

The first and foremost priority for a psychic empath is having good shields that meet your individual needs. You should start with those first, but while you're in the process of building them up, there are other techniques that you can learn to use to control, limit or cut off energetic emotional input as needed. And those are in the next chapter....

Seven
Protecting Your Personal Energy

In the last chapter, we talked about energetic shields for the empath – how to build them, how to adjust them to our individual needs, and how to set them up so their intensity can either be set by conscious choice or adapt automatically to the specific circumstances around us, depending on what we need most at any time.

Whew! We covered a lot of ground.

Now that we have all of these techniques, next we'll look at an assortment of other ways to control energy. You can use these methods to control how much emotional energy you take in, decrease your intake to levels you can deal with, or even cut it off (if the energy is too negative or overwhelming). There are many ways to protect your own emotional energy from the overwhelming emotions of others, especially in intense situations such as crowds, crisis, or confrontation. It's good to learn them now, especially before you actually need them.

To understand how these techniques work, you need to understand psychic perception. In chapter one, we talked about the different types of psychic ability.

- Clairvoyants "see things"/ have visions.
- Clairaudients "hear things".
- Clairsentients "just know things".
- Folks perceiving psychically through smell or taste,
- And people who feel things, including people who get information from objects (psychometrists) and people sensitive to emotional vibrations (empaths).

Each sensory system is found in a different part of the body.

- The center for clairvoyance is just between and above

your eyes on your forehead, in the area called the third eye;

- The center for clairaudience is on either side of the head, just above the ears;
- The center for clairsentience is in the crown and the top of the head;
- The center for psychic perception by smell is the nose;
- The center for psychic perception by taste is in the mouth, especially on the tongue;
- The center for psychometry is in the hands:
  And, finally
- The center for psychic empathy is in the stomach, abdomen, and solar plexus.

Yes, you did read that right. Your stomach.

Ever wonder why people talk about having a "gut reaction"? That "gut reaction" is your psychic empathy in action, giving you the information that you cannot access through your other five senses. You get a "gut reaction", when input comes through the empathic psychic sensory system in your abdomen. You get "butterflies in your stomach" when your empathy is giving you the heads up that something is wrong, even though consciously you haven't figured out what's happening yet. You "find your center" to become stable and focused. You "trust your gut". You access your "inner wisdom".

You may not have realized it, but many common phrases related to instinct and intuition are based on the energetic sensory center for psychic empathy. Though most people are not aware of psychic ability and how it works, the effects of the empathic sensory system are so noticeable that sayings and folklore have grown up around them.

Why's it important to know this? Because, once we know

that most of the empathic input comes in through our middle, we can use techniques that cover, protect or shield that area of our body to gain more control over what and how much energy we allow into ourselves.

While we're at it, here's another point worth knowing. As said above, the empathic psychic sensory center is based in the stomach, abdomen, and solar plexus. For a psychic empath with limited or no control of her gift, her body may protect itself in an unusual way. Psychic empaths with little control of energetic input tend to gain weight in abdomen and tummy. This extra padding serves as an extra layer of insulation or armor, slowing down the input of emotional energy and helping the beginning empath to cope with the energy around her.

(Ever had problems losing or keeping off abdominal weight? This may be a cue to you that you need to work on having better energetic control. So crunch those shields....)

Now that we know about the sensory center for empathic energy, we can go on and look at techniques for controlling energetic input.

And, the first and foremost technique is that, if the energy around you is too overwhelming, too negative, too powerful, the best way to deal with this is to remove yourself from the situation that's too much for you.

Just that. Walk away.

Staying in a situation which is too much for you is like pounding your head against a wall. You can keep doing it if you like, but it won't get you anywhere.

So, if you can leave the room, leave the area, stop spending time with the creators of major drama, you can take a lot of weight off of yourself.

There are times though when you can't just side step the energetically overloading situation. At that point, you need other ways to manage the energy around you.

Caught in a negative work space? Dealing with an obnoxious relative or pushy neighbor? Caring for someone who's seriously ill, or very depressed? Is the person you love really annoyed with you? The energy around you is negative, but you may not be able to walk away from it.

The next best option is to do what you can to maintain your personal space. Personal space is open space around you that you need to feel comfortable. It's largest for strangers, smaller for acquaintances, and closest for close friends and people you love.

For empaths, the closer a person is, the more effect that person's energy has on the empath. The strongest energetic effect is when a person is actually touches you.

So, if the energy is stressful, and you can't walk away now, the next best thing is to put what space you can between you and the person creating the problem energy.

If the person is touching you, shift your position slightly so that you are no longer touching. If she's in your personal space, take a step or two away. Find a reason to move to a more comfortable, formal distance, without seeming like you're turning and running.

Increasing your space will decrease the energetic load you are carrying, and give you more comfort so that you can get your center back.

One thing you can do to control how much energy you take in is lay the groundwork in advance.

Did you know that some of the things that you eat can

help you gain control of your empathy?

Caffeine tends to increase the speed of our reaction to input around us. With appropriate caffeine, energy comes in like a slow ball as opposed to a fast ball, and is easier to manage. And sugar, in all forms, gives us the energy we need to deal more easily with whatever comes.

(Related to this, we'll talk about how meat and oily foods help ground out negative energy in a future chapter.).

So, keep in mind that choosing what kind of things you eat and drink can make you better able to control your interaction with the energy around you.

Want another way to control how much energy you take in when someone sends negative energy your way?

Just stand sideways.

As you recall, the empathic sensory system is based in your stomach, abdomen and solar plexus. This means that, if you face someone when she puts out massive waves of anger, fear or depression, all of that energy has a direct route into that abdominal center and then into your body. If, on the other hand, you turn so you're at right angles to that same person, you'll find that the volume on that energy is cranked way down, and that you experience far less of it.

The position that you want (if you must stay in that situation) is to shift your weight until you are at right angles to the source, with your head turned sideways so that you are still making eye contact while protecting your solar plexus. This is polite to the person you're with, while still taking care of yourself energetically.

You can try this for yourself. Wait for a situation when you're receiving a lot of emotional energy, preferably positive energy, from a single person. Face her full on.

Stop and pay attention to what your body tells you. How much energy are you receiving? How does it feel?

Now turn your body slightly away, so that your abdomen is angled away from your subject, while you continue to look at her. Feel the difference? How does it feel? Can you feel how changing the angle of your body helps you control the amount of energy you're exposed to?

This is a good technique to practice when there is a lot of positive energy. Practicing can help build this in as a habit so that, if your situation becomes challenging, you'll adjust your position automatically, rather than be overwhelmed by explosive energy around you.

There's another way to use the empathic sensory center to control how much emotional energy you take in.

Just cover your tummy or solar plexus.

No, really…

Ever notice how, when people are open to things, their arms and legs are uncrossed? And when they're closed, they tend to fold their arms and legs? There's a point to this.…

Unconsciously, people "closed" to a person or idea are shutting off any aspects of it that might apply pressure or influence on them on its behalf. That includes emotional energetic pressure…

This is another method you should try for yourself under conditions of positive energy, as it'll be easier on you and more conducive to seeing how it works. Pick a time when you're receiving a lot of emotional energy, preferably positive, from a single person. Face her full on.

Pay attention to what your body says. How much energy are you receiving? How does it make you feel?

Now cross your arms so that they lie low on your chest, overshadowing your solar plexus. Can you feel a difference when you do this? How does it feel to you? Can you feel how covering your solar plexus helps you control the amount of emotional energy you are exposed to?

This works with both arms crossed, or with one arm crossed and the other arm up in the "chin thoughtfully in hand" position. The "one arm up, other arm crossed' combines nicely with the "turning to the side" technique that we discussed in the previous section of this chapter. If you practice this position in advance, it looks perfectly normal and natural. It also works well combined with a way of cutting off excess energy coming in the next chapter   .

This is another technique to practice in times when there's a lot of positive energy. Practicing builds this as a habit so that it becomes automatic in times of stress.

There are other ways to shield your sensory center. Moving behind a counter. Sitting behind a desk. Standing behind podium or pulpit. Any of these offer more coverage, and more control of the energy you're exposed to.

And finally, you can set an intention. If you recall from chapter three, an intention is just a thought that sets a concrete definition for what you want to happen. So set an intention that you only take in as much emotional energy as you can deal with at any particular time, and no more so.

The intention uses the mind-body connection to co-ordinate shields, sensitivity and other skills and techniques to control how much energy you take in.

When you are trying to control the amount of emotional energy that you are taking in, you can use any of these techniques. You can also use more than one of them, either in sequence or in combination.

- You can turn slightly away and fold your arms;
- You can change your angle and take two steps back.
- You can fold your arms until you come up with a good reason to excuse yourself and leave the area.

What's important is that you have many tools you can use to have more control over interaction with energy around you.

Eight
Separating from Other People's Energy

We've talked about energetic shields, and how they can help us keep our own personal energy distinct and separate from the energy of other people around us.

We've talked about methods and techniques to control or limit the amount of energy we take in from the ambient energy around us.

But there are going to be times when having shields and knowing how to protect your personal energy from the energy flowing around you may not be enough. Times when people around you are really angry, really depressed, or really upset. Times when there is more energy being thrown at you than your shields and your techniques for controlling energy may be able to handle. Times when you cannot immediately leave the area.

There may even be times when people are not only attacking you verbally, but also energetically by "shouting" at you with their energy (consciously or unconsciously).

.   And times when you are accused of being "over-sensitive" because the average person does not perceive the psychic assault accompanying the verbal or physical one.

At times like these, you may need to take more decisive steps to actually break away from the energy you're receiving.

That's what we're going to look at next.

When you're facing a situation of extreme energetic input, it can become vibrationally attached to you. It can latch into you, leaving you hooked like a fish on a line. That energetic line not only funnels more and more of that overwhelming energy into you, but also makes it hard for you to detach yourself from the source of the energy.

This is a situation where someone else's energy is running roughshod right over you; and where you're stuck in that situation.

At this point, you may want to use the techniques in this

chapter for cutting the connection this energy has made with you. Severing the connection, so you're no longer being overwhelmed by the emotional energy.

There's one thing you must keep in mind about these particular techniques. They're only good to interrupt the problematic energy flow temporarily.

The purpose of these particular techniques is not to permanently resolve the energetic situation. The purpose of these techniques is to interrupt the overwhelming flow of energy temporarily so you have space enough to regain your center, and breathing room enough to do something more permanent about the situation.

Time to:

- Take a deep breath;
- Realize what's happening to you;
- Regain your composure;
- Turn sideways;
- Upgrade your shields;
- Take a step or two back;
- Cover your energetic emotional sensory system;
  Or,
- Leave the situation altogether.

It's not enough to use these techniques to disengage from overwhelming energy. If you're going to use one of these methods, you need to also know what your immediate next step is after you've disengaged from the energy flow.

You do the technique to disengage - and you do your follow-up procedure as fast as possible thereafter.

And, if you can, remove yourself from the problem altogether.

The definition of insanity is to keep doing the same thing and expect different results. When you're faced with overwhelming energy hooking into your energy field, you need to disengage, and then change your approach. If you don't change what you're doing, the negative energy will reattach itself. Techniques for disengaging will not fix the problem here, but they do interrupt the cycle and give you the chance to break free of it.

As said in previous chapters, the sensory system for empathic reception is located in your stomach, abdomen and solar plexus. We've talked about different ways to shield or protect this area to limit or control energy coming in through it.

If you have an extra strong flow of overwhelming empathic energy coming in through this area, you may need to take more emphatic steps.

One of the best ways to interrupt incoming energy is to pass your hand or arm briskly between the sensory area and the source of the energy.

Picture a kind of karate chop passing over stomach and abdomen. Your hand or forearm can pass briskly over your sensory center, moving downwards or upwards, depending on which is more convenient for you. As you make this movement, set your intention that all energy coming in through your empathic sensory center is cut off completely at that moment.

As you do your "chop", set your intention that the "chop" interrupts and severs incoming energy, disengaging you from it so that you can take other steps.

This may sound like it might look a little odd in public. Not necessarily. This is not the kind of "chop" that requires flare and a martial arts yell. There are several ways you can do it that are less obtrusive.

- You can raise your hand to sneeze, push up your glasses, or scratch your head, passing over your abdomen in the process.

- Remember the position with one arm crossed over your solar plexus, and your chin resting in the other hand? You can take the hand holding your chin and drop it to your side, crossing the abdomen.
- You can also raise that hand from your side to hold that chin.
- You can accompany a firm "No!" with crossing both arms in front of you, covering the sensory center, and then moving them briskly outwards.
- You can use the gesture to accompany casual conversation.

There are lots of variations of this gesture you can do as part of normal everyday life.

Remember, this only temporarily cuts off energy -

So:
- Chop and turn;
- Chop and step back;
- Chop and turn up your shields;
  Or
- Chop, excuse yourself and walk away...

An energetic chop is a practical option. You always have the tools with you that you need to do it.

If, a chop is not viable for some reason, there's another way to cut off energy.

One thing the psychological and the metaphysical world hold in common is the use of symbolism. As noted in chapter three, in both worlds, the symbol is the thing, and, through the mind-body connection, the use of symbols can have a very genuine effect on the actual nature of reality.

So, if you want to cut off excess energy input, what do you need?

You need something that cuts.

- A knife;
- A pair of scissors;
- A sword:

Anything at all that you can picture working to cut off negative energy and sever the connection between you and the energy's source.

You can visualize your cutting implement severing the excess energy flow, and giving you the chance to close your energy field against the overwhelm. This works well in public, where waving a machete around only makes people uncomfortable.

In the privacy of your own home, you can also use an actual cutting tool, such as a pair of scissors, Sometimes, using a physical tool gives your visualization additional strength and power, and this can be especially helpful when dealing with a long term case of negative energy.

Set things up so you have privacy to concentrate. Picture the negative energy connection with your empathic sensory center, and then carefully cut through the air in front of your abdomen, symbolically "cutting the connection". You may feel energetic improvement as you do this.

Whether you choose to do it with visualized or actual tools, visualizing cutting this energetic connection can help you break free of the more serious energetic overload.

Finally, before leaving the topic of disconnecting from

overwhelming or aggressive energy, let's review.

Whether you use a "chop" or symbolically cut aggressive energy, remember you need to follow the detach with some other approach to be sure that you stay unattached.

Use the techniques for what they're meant for- strategic withdrawal – and then move to other methods for long term solutions.

Nine
Energetic House Cleaning-
Clearing, Grounding and Releasing Unwanted Energy

We've talked about different types of energetic shields, to create energetic space that's yours alone;

We've talked about energetic techniques to keep a space between your energy and that of other people;

We've talked about ways to actively disengage from aggressive or overwhelming energy sent your way;

We've talked about how sometimes you have to leave a situation of overwhelming energy altogether;

But what happens when, despite good intentions and these techniques, negative energy gets into your personal energetic field and sets up housekeeping?

Then, you need to "ground out" negative energy.

If we have all of this knowledge and all of these wonderful techniques to keep our energy separate from that of other people, why would we even have to deal with grounding out negative energy?

Well, even with the best knowledge and the strongest shields in the cosmos, eventually there will come a time when some of the bad stuff will sneak on through....

- When someone you trust blows up without warning;
- When you're working with the chronically physically or mentally ill;
- When you're caught in a rapidly escalating situation, like a riot or a violent crime;
- When you're ill, injured, or in pain;
- When you work in a climate of corporate paranoia;
- When someone explodes near you unexpectedly;
- During a personal crisis;

- Due to a pattern of ongoing stress, which gradually wears down your innate natural resilience;

Or any other negative or explosive situation that takes you by surprise.

It's worth noting that not all negative energy comes from outside of you. Some negative energy is a "do-it-yourself" project, and, if it lingers, that kind of energy can drain you as badly as external negative energy can.

No matter what you do, you'll sometimes end up carrying around your own or someone else's negative, cranky, or blue energy. This is why you need to know how to ground this energy out safely; how to let negative energy go its way rather than build up inside you.

In the next chapter, we'll talk about how to keep your own personal energy positive, but first, in this chapter, we'll talk about how to ground out either kind of negative energy, so that you can release it and let it go.

Let's start by noting that, even if you're carrying around a lot of excess, negative or "stuck" energy, you may not be able to ground it all out right away.

Being empaths, we automatically tend to pick up a lot of energy that isn't ours; but some of the surplus energy that we're carrying is in our bodies or energy fields for a reason- a good reason.

Sometimes, it's with us because it's there to teach us something, tell us something, or show us something; and we may not be able to release it until we've understood what that something is.

Sometimes we're not *ready* to release all of it yet....

The grounding techniques in this chapter are all effective. Since different people have different needs, you may find some of them suit your particular temperament and situation better than others, but it's good to be familiar with them all, in case your needs, or preferences change; and even the best of these techniques may not be able to ground out all of the energy you are carrying if you've still got some business to finish with it.

So, if you're doing energy grounding but have some energy that won't seem to let go, you should probably stop for a moment or two, and look to see if that energy has a message for you. If there's something that you need to hear, or change, or learn, or do.

Then ground out the energy again.

And watch it go on its merry way....

What's this energetic grounding stuff anyway? And how does it work?

In metaphysics, "grounding" can mean two different (but not mutually exclusive) things.

One type of grounding strengthens a psychic's connection with the physical world. When a person does a lot of psychic work (how much qualifies as "a lot" varies from person to person), his connection with his body and the physical world itself can become weaker, as he reaches out energetically to connect with non-physical space. The simple act of energetically grounding can strengthen or reestablish the physical connection for the psychic.

The other use for energetic grounding (the one that is more immediately important to we empaths here) is to drain old, overwhelming, negative or "stuck" energy out of us, returning it to the Earth with the intention that it will be recycled into something beneficial to the world. Mother Earth is certainly powerful enough to take this energy without being harmed by it, and to change negative energy into something positive, especially if we use our intention to help Her...

Think of it as being like energetic spring cleaning...

Energetic grounding can help you keep your personal energy clear on those days when protecting your energetic field is just not enough to do the job.

Most of the exercises in this chapter can be used to do either kind of grounding, with only a change in intent to select the purpose. We're primarily going to be focusing on the function of clearing out any negative energy that we don't need to hold on to any more.

In most of these exercises, I'll be talking about grounding our energy into the earth. Let's discuss that for a minute.

In metaphysics, some people see the earth as a planet. Some people see the earth as a primordial force. Some people see the earth as a being, far bigger and more powerful than we are. Some people see the earth as a goddess. Some people see the earth as a charge to be protected and nurtured. And some people view the earth as a power quite capable of caring for Herself, and us as well.

Wow. That's a lot of ways of seeing the earth, no? It's not my job to say how you see the Earth. That's something you must decide for yourself.

But, no matter how each of us sees the Earth, there are still a few things we all can agree on...

- That the Earth is powerful, no matter how you see it;
- That the Earth is very good at transmuting things from one state into another, and at recycling things into a more beneficial form;
- That intentions can shape the nature of reality around us, and that a positive intention can help the Earth to do what She is good at;
- And that gratitude is also powerful, and can contribute significantly to positive outcomes we seek.

(Say what? Where on Earth did that last bit come from?...)

There's a couple of good reasons why the emotional

energy of gratitude is important as part of any life, but it's especially important in one involving energetic issues.

First, from a pure energetic standpoint, positive energy tends to attract positive people, experiences and things. Negative energy tends to attract more negative people, experiences and things.

Per the Law of Attraction, like calls to like, so if you're trying to manifest a more positive reality, positive emotions, such as gratitude, are at least helpful and at most essential. You need that positive energy to attract a more positive reality, and to build the necessary state of positive expectation that you can actually attain that better world.

So your mother was right- it's actually very helpful and practical to count your blessings.

Let's look at this from the standpoint of courtesy.

Whether you see the Earth as a planet, a powerful force, a being, a goddess, or you're not sure yet, think of this- what you're doing when you ground energy into the Earth is saying that:

- you have a burden too heavy for you to bear;
- asking someone or thing more powerful then you to take it over for you; and
- turning your burden over to that powerful other.

Now, at that point, don't you think a "Thank You" is appropriate?

Without gratitude, grounding energy can be like littering - dropping your waste and running away.

With gratitude and the intention that the negative energy will be transformed into something more positive for the world around you, this becomes a collaboration between you and the

Earth, where everyone wins.

It's respectful. And respect is part of a good working relationship.

(Don't get me wrong. Mother Earth is certainly strong enough to take care of business with or without a person's intention. But for each of us to help as best we can, according to our own strength and skills, builds a stronger, healthier partnership, which is better for all of us, including the Earth.)

And that having been said - on to the exercises!

The first and easiest thing we can do to ground out negative energy is to eat.

That's right - eat. Not too hard, that....

Eating tends to increase our connection with our body and the physical world. Especially if we're eating something that we really enjoy.

And eating meat, or oily or fatty foods is helpful in grounding out excess energy.

If you recall from chapter seven:

- caffeine increases your reaction speed to energy (making it easier to deal with before it affects you); and,
- sugar gives you the energy to deal with situations without being overwhelmed.

Combine this with fatty food's ability to help you ground out excess energy, and that makes chocolate as close to a perfect food for empaths as you can get....

Well, that explains a lot....

Now, I'm not saying that, to manage your empathic energy, all you have to do is to sit around eating truffles; but these foods can help you to strike a better energetic balance. At that point, it's useful to know how they affect your energy and your body, and use them in moderation as part of your system of energy maintenance.

(And isn't it nice that a piece of chocolate can be a key part of that plan?...)

Another way of clearing out negative energy is to breathe it out. Breath work can be very powerful in shifting or clearing energy, and it has the added bonus that it doesn't require any special equipment.

Any type of meditation, including breath work, boils down to focusing exclusively on an item or an experience and screening out other sensory input. Meditating for a significant amount of time, such as a half an hour a day can have significant positive effects on your energy, health, and well-being, but even a small amount (as little as five minutes) can be of benefit.

For best results, before doing any kind of meditation, you need to arrange your situation so you can focus on it without distractions.

So send your family out to the movies or the circus. Lock the door and draw the drapes. Shut down your email, and take the phone off of the hook. Get ready to spend some time exclusively with yourself and with your meditation practice.

Breathing Meditation for Clearing Negative Energy

Settle yourself in your chair with your arms and legs uncrossed. Adjust your body until you're comfortable. Close your eyes, and relax.

Begin paying attention to your breathing, Listen to how you breathe in and breathe out, breathe in and breathe out.

Don't try to change or affect how you breathe, just focus your attention in a relaxed manner on your breathing. How you breathe in and breathe out, breathe in and breathe out.

Don't try to change or affect how you breathe. Just focus your attention in a relaxed manner on your breathing, how you breathe in and breathe out, breathe in and breathe out, breathe in and breathe out, and focus only on your breathing.....

And, as you breathe, and as you focus on your breathing, expand your focus to become aware of your body and energy field, and how your energy is held safely and securely around you inside of your energetic shields. Focus on your body and your energetic field.

And as you focus on your body and your energetic field, become aware of any negative energy you're holding in your body or energetic field, whether energy from emotions belonging to others or from your own negative emotions. Become aware of where you are holding that energy, whether it is in your neck or back or stomach or any other portion of your body or of your energy field swirling around you.

And now that you are aware of the negative energy that you are holding onto, and of how it is affecting you, return your attention to your breathing. Picture the air that you are breathing in and out as being filled with energy and Light, brilliant, sparkling, filled with positive potential.

And when you breathe out, see yourself releasing and breathing out negative energy you've been holding, releasing it and breathing it out of your body, out of your life. Set your intention that, as you breathe out the negative energy, it is gathered up and returned to Mother Earth. Intend that the negative energy will all be transformed into something positive that will be of benefit to the world around you.

Notice how your body changes as the negative energy is released and carried away. Remember the way your body felt when it was carrying that negative emotion, so that, if you start to accumulate negative emotional energy again, you'll know the symptoms that indicate that you need to clear it once more.

And when you breathe in, picture yourself breathing in that energy, that Light. Let it fill the spaces left open and empty by releasing the negative energy. Let it flood your body with Light.

Breathe out the negative energy that you have been holding onto, and breathe in the Light. Keep visualizing this until the last bit of negative energy is gone, and the Light has filled your body and spilled over to fill your energy field as well.

And when your body and energetic field are clear of negative energy, when your body is filled with Light, and when you are ready to come back, return your attention to the room and slowly, slowly open your eyes...

The more that you practice this breathing exercise, the easier it becomes to clear out negative energy by using it. If you practice it regularly, eventually you'll be able to clear a certain amount of energy on the fly, immediately after energetically challenging situations (which is certainly a useful skill to have).

And now, on to the next grounding technique.

In the metaphysical world, one of the key rules of working is "the symbol is the thing". An item or activity that is symbolic of something else can give you a handle to affect that other thing.

How does that help us? We want to clear our bodies and energy fields of negative energy, right? So, we're going to ground it out by washing that energy away. And one of the easiest ways is just to go and wash your hands.

Running water has been a patent remedy against negative energy and bad things for as long as folks have been recording this sort of information. We're going to use that symbolic cleansing to clear our energy field.

Just been through an acrimonious meeting at work, or stuck in a car pool with nasty people?

Head for the bathroom. Turn the faucets on. As the water runs over your hands, close your eyes and picture the water rushing over and through your energy field, washing away all negative or "stuck" energy, and leaving your own energy clean and clear.

As you wash your hands, set an intention that all negative energy that you are ready to release is pulled out of your body through your hands and washed away permanently. Set an intention that it is recycled by the Earth into something positive, to the benefit to all.

As noted in chapter two, you have energy centers in the palms of your hands known as "chakras". There are also chakras in the soles of your feet, the crown of your head, the base of your spine, and down the midline of the front and back of your body. Whether moving energy into or out of your body, it's easier to do through your chakras.

And here, you are washing out excess, negative or "stuck" energy through the chakras in your palms.

This is a quick and easy clearing, and one that you can do as part of your normal routine. (Indeed, even if you're having a good day, you may well wish to do this each time you wash your hands, to keep excess emotional energy from piling up.)

(See, your mother was right. If you want to keep from getting sick, you do need to wash those hands.)

Next on our expanding collection of methods to ground out negative energy is an environmental approach.

That's right. We're going to hug a tree…

Remember the metaphysical concept "the symbol is the thing" we talked about in the last exercise?

Plants excel at recycling and transformation, taking in carbon dioxide and putting out oxygen. All plants, trees in particular, have deep roots, grounding them firmly into the earth. Trees are strong and solid. Energetically, trees combine the best elements of strength, transformation, and grounding, with their own powerful energetic fields.

Feeling frazzled because of too much energy. Carrying a bunch of negative energy around with you?

Then it's time to take a walk in Nature…

Pick an area with a wide assortment of trees for your walk, and look around for a tree that attracts you. Once you and your tree have chosen each other, you're going to want to have physical contract with it so that it can help you to ground out the negative or excess emotional energy. The most effective way of moving energy out of your body is through the chakras that run down the midline of the front and the back of your body.

If the area is more private or you're not worried about what people think if they see you, you may wish to stand facing the tree and hug it closely. If you're in a more public area, it's also fairly effective to sit with your back leaning firmly against the tree.

Grounding Out Energy Through a Tree

Once you're comfortably in position, close your eyes. Concentrate and become aware of your energy field and that of the tree that is helping you. Identify the areas of excess, negative, or "stuck" energy that you're carrying.

Now, breathe out, picturing the energy passing out of your body and energy field, into the tree, and then down and out of the tree's roots into the earth. Set an intention that the energy will be transformed into something more positive that will be of benefit to the world.

Continue to breathe until you feel that you've cleared all of the unwanted energy, or until you feel that you have cleared as much energy that you're ready to release at this time.

Send a feeling of gratitude to this tree and to the earth for their help. Then, slowly, open your eyes.

This is best done with a tree, as it is a living being with its own energy field that may help you to ground. Sometimes, however, there isn't a tree around. At that point, a vertical metal support beam has many of the characteristics needed for this method.

Besides having chakras (energy vortexes) down the midline of our bodies, we also have them in the base of our spines, the top of our heads, the palms of our hands and the soles of our feet.

The term "grounding" refers to making firm energetic contact with the earth, and moving out negative energy through this connection. The chakras in the soles of our feet are great for grounding.

How can you ground through the chakras in the soles of your feet?

You can stomp. Dance vigorously. March. Tap dance. Hike. Boogaloo. Do anything that brings your feet in firm contact with the earth.

As you make this contact, picture any excess, negative, or "stuck" energy being stomped out of the soles of your feet and into the earth, where your intention helps it to be transformed into something more positive for the world around you.

So go ahead,

Put on your dancing shoes,

And ground out unnecessary energy.

We've grounded through the chakras on the midline of our bodies, front and back. We've grounded through the chakras in our hands and our feet. So how about grounding through the chakra at the base of our spine?

I've got a good method – but it may look silly.

Grounding Energy While Sitting

Sit in a chair with your legs uncrossed and your feet planted firmly on the floor.

Close your eyes and picture roots coming spiraling out of the base of your spine, spiraling outwards and downwards, reaching downwards until they root firmly into the core of the Earth. Then press against the ground with your feet and bounce gently up and down in your seat.

As you bounce, picture all negative energy being moved downwards with every bounce, downwards out of your body and through your energetic roots until it reaches the core of the earth and stays there. Set an intention for the energy to be transformed into something more positive for the world around you.

And, when you've grounded out as much negative energy as you can at this time, open your eyes.

This exercise can feel silly, but it works really well for energetically grounding. It doesn't have to look outrageous either. With a bit of practice, you can use it to ground with even subtle "bounces", which makes it a good choice for grounding in such situations as acrimonious meetings, family gatherings, and on public transportation.

Let's see now. In the course of working our way through our toolbox of energetic grounding techniques, we have taken our excess, negative or "stuck" energy and sent it into the ground. We have washed it away with water. We have breathed it out with air.

Thinking of this, that's three out of four elements.

And the fourth and final element is ...FIRE.

Fire is a traditional cleanser, clearer, and transformer of great power, having the ability to shift a majority of things, including energy of all kinds, from one state to another with ease. In nature, fire burns away the old plantings, making room for new growth. Energetically, fire can also burn away "stuck" energy, and all energy we are carrying that we no longer need anymore, making room for healing and for Light. Fire wipes the slate clean, and prepares us to freely start again.

So let us see how taking our problem energy and grounding it out into fire works for us.

Fire is trickier to work with than other elements. It's potentially more dangerous if not treated with respect. Fire is not the enemy, but you must take care with it.

When working with fire, you have a number of options. You can gaze into a camp fire. You can stare at a candle lantern. You can light a fire in the fire place. You can start a tiny flame in a cast iron brazier.

When I'm working with fire, I like to use a candle, and, for safety's sake, my primary preference is a candle housed in a candle cup or jar. This shelters the flame from breezes, so it won't blow out or over and set something on fire. I like a candle cup with a broad flat base, so that the candle is stable. I also prefer to put the candle on an uncluttered, non-flammable counter or table, so it's not near anything that it can scorch or torch; and near a sink, so I can soak things down if need be.

Maybe that's being overly cautious. But I've done a lot of fire work, and I haven't set the Universe on fire yet...

Be aware that, while you are doing this exercise, you will be breathing energy into the flame. To avoid extinguishing the flame while you breathe, you need to either shelter the flame from your breath (as in a candle cup or candle lantern), or position yourself far enough away from the flame source so that your breath does not directly blow on or extinguish the flame.

When you work with fire, you need all of the preparation that you do for other meditations, plus arranging things so that no one will walk into, tip over or be set alight by your source of fire. Just as with previous meditations, you need to arrange your situation so that you can focus on meditation without distractions.

Let anyone who shares your space with you know what you are doing, so that they won't accidentally end up walking in and setting themselves on fire. If you can clear the space of other people for your exclusive working or if you can involve them in the process by showing them how to clear their own unwanted energy, that's all the better. If you have pets, see that they are secured in a different area, so they will not distract you, or tip over the flame. Shut down the phone, the computer, and your email. Draw the drapes and close doors for the minimum distractions possible. Set up your space so you're ready to exclusively focus on yourself and your grounding fire meditation.

Place your candle or other source of fire on a clear, stable, nonflammable table or counter, where it will burn safely, stay upright, and not be within reach of anything flammable. Arrange things so you have a place to sit, stand or lie in a comfortable position while still being able to see the source of the flame. Light the candle or fire source.

Position yourself so you're comfortable but can still see the flame easily. You should be positioned with arms and legs uncrossed, in a comfortable position so you can focus on your fire meditation and not be distracted by your body. If you have a tendency to nod off or to fall asleep when lying down, a seated or standing position would be a better choice for you while you do this meditation.

Whew! That's a lot of preparations and precautions! Please don't get intimidated, though. This technique is pleasant, effective and simple, and all of the instructions up to this point are designed to keep your experience that way and safe besides (rather than having to call the fire department, or having an outrageous sit com experience that you can tell your children about years from now…)

Are you comfortable? Then we're ready to begin.

Grounding Energy Through Fire.

Close your eyes and focus on your breathing. Breathe in and breathe out, breathe in and breathe out. As you breathe, softly shift your attention to your body. Focus on your body and notice any tension in it. Notice where your body holds its tension, in neck or back or jaw.

And as you breathe in and breathe out, see yourself breathing relaxation into those places of tension you noted. Feel your breath relaxing the tension, and, as you breathe out, picture yourself breathing the tension out of your body, and away from you.

Breathe in relaxation and breathe out tension, until your body is totally and completely relaxed.

And now that you're completely relaxed, turn your attention once more to your body, and to your energy field surrounding your body inside of your energetic shields.

Focus on your body and your energy field, and find out where you are holding excess, or negative, or "stuck" energy inside of you.

You may see this unwanted energy as patches of distortion or of color, color that is more muddy in tone or significantly different and less attractive to you than the rest of your energetic field. You may feel it as tension, or vibration, or any other "off" feeling that does not match the rest of your energy. You may hear it as a discordant note, or unpleasant sound. You may just know where the energy in your body or your energetic field is just not quite right.

Once you've located the excessive, negative or "stuck" energy in your body or energy field, you're ready to ground it out through fire.

Open your eyes now. Open them slowly, still holding your awareness of the unwanted energy and your energy field as you look at your source of fire.

Look at the flame. Look deeply into it. See how it dances and flickers, steady yet constantly changing.

Set your intention that you are going to project all of the excessive, negative or "stuck" energy out of your body and your energy field, and into the flame. Set an intention at this point that the energy will be burned up by the flame, and transmuted into something positive for the greater good of the world around you.

Continue to deeply breathe in and breathe out. Picture that unwanted energy is easily released from your body and energetic field; and expelled as you breathe out. Picture the energy being carried by your breath out of your body and energy field, and into the flame that you have lit.

Watch what happens to the flame, as you breathe out unneeded energy. Do you see any changes in it? When I do this technique, many times I have seen the flame begin to change in color or size, crackle audibly or flicker when I send the excess energy into it. When I stopped sending energy into the flame, it returned to its regular state.

Continue to breathe deeply and to release the excessive, negative or "stuck" energy until you have cleared yourself of all of it, or at least as much energy as you are currently ready and able to release.

Once you're done, be sure to extinguish the flame. Don't leave a flame burning unattended. In metaphysics, it's considered more appropriate to extinguish a candle with a snuffer or the flame proof lid of a brazier, rather than blowing it out.

Over the years, when I have had more severe cases of negative energy overload, I have found that the judicious use of fire is one of the best ways available to clear the energetic decks and start fresh once again. Fire is both very powerful and soothing to the psyche, and can leave you feeling cleared in body, mind and spirit.

We've just worked on grounding energetically with fire. Let's go back to the opposite element – water.

Remember how, earlier in this chapter, we used washing your hands as an impromptu way of grounding out excess, negative or "stuck" energy on the fly?

Well, that's a method that has a lot going for it. It's:

- quick;
- easy;
- discrete;
- effective;
- accessible to you under most situations;
- only requires equipment that is generally available;
- gives you a reason to withdraw from overwhelming situations;
- a method that you can do when you need to, without causing people to ask questions;
- something that you can repeat as often as you like without any significant side effects (other than dry or prune-y hands, of course....)

There are a lot of good aspects to this grounding technique. One of the best things about it is that you can easily kick this technique up to the next level.

Energetic cleansing on a regular basis can keep excess, negative or "stuck" energy from building up to unhealthy, uncomfortable or dysfunctional levels. It's good to make emotional energetic cleansing part of your daily routine. One way is making it a part of a shower.

Grounding by washing your hands combines the symbolism of cleansing of the element of water with the chakras (energy vortexes) in the palms of your hands. You visualize releasing and grounding out unwanted energy. The water rushing over your hands draws the energy out of through your chakras and washes it away.

You've got two chakras in your hands, one in each palm. You've got many more located throughout your entire body. Why not use them to your best advantage?

You don't need to make special arrangements or preparations for a shower intended to ground out unwanted energy. Feel free to make some if you like, though. As human beings, we are creatures of habit and ritual; and, repetition can help to make energetic working easier. (Just like everything else, practice makes perfect.)

If every time that you take a shower for grounding out energy, you use the same scent of soap, put on music in the background, or recite an affirmation or poem before you get into the shower, you'll find repeating these cues for future showers makes the whole process easier, faster and more effective. With repetition, you smell the shampoo or hear the music, and your energy becomes conditioned to slip automatically into the altered state you need to do the energetic work...

Or... you can pass on the sensory cues. They can certainly help you move into an altered state, but the only things you truly need for this process are yourself, water, and your own intention.

Grounding Out Negative Energy in the Shower

When it's time for a shower, and you want to make grounding out unwanted energy part of your routine, begin by setting an intention before getting into the shower itself.

- Set an intention to release, clear and ground out all energy that you're ready to let go of now.
- Set an intention that all of the energy that you release will be washed away down the drain, and, from there, into the earth.
- Set an intention that all of the grounded out energy will be transformed into something that is positive and beneficial for the world around you.
- Set an intention that release of energy is easy and pleasant, and that you feel great once you're done.
- Set an intention that you remember to ground out any unwanted energy each time that you shower.
- Set the intentions that support you achieving what you want to accomplish in a way as positive, simple, automatic and empowering as possible.

The power of intention is what alters reality around you and sets instructions for what's going to happen energetically. Setting an intention before you start to work, and holding it in your mind as you do your process (such as showering) determines what is going to happen.

Once you're in the shower, position yourself under the running water. Close your eyes for a minute, and focus your awareness on your body and your energy field.

Focus on how your body feels. Note any places of tension or pain. (Many times, these sensations are signs of places where unwanted energy is held.) Look for other places where you may be holding onto this energy.

Next, expand your awareness to your energy field. Check if there are places in your field that you're holding any unwanted or outmoded energy. (Energy sometimes lodges in your energy field for awhile before moving inwards into your body.)

Once you've connected with your body and energy field and located any unwanted energy, remain aware of that energy but shift your focus to the water as it pours over you. Feel the power of the water, and how it washes over every part of you.

As you wash your body, picture yourself also washing your energy field. Sudsing up your psyche. Scrubbing "stuck" energy loose. Washing away unwanted emotional energy to let your own clear, clean, beautiful personal energy shine through.

Next, picture the water as full of Light- Light that has the power needed to wash away anything negative, dysfunctional or harmful to you. Feel the Light pouring over your body and through your energetic field, washing away all energy that you are ready, willing and able to release now. Feel the unwanted energy being washed down the drain. Picture it passing to a stream, a river, and then an ocean, before passing into the earth and being transmuted into something more positive for the world.

Picture the Light continuing to fall, and filling up space formerly filled by the unwanted energy, so there is no place left for that negative energy to creep back into.

Finally, focus on your body and your energy field again. Notice what your body feels like when clean and clear of negative energy; and what your energy field feels like when it is no longer carrying unwanted energy.

Knowing what your body and your energy field feel like when they are in a better condition helps you to be more aware of when you pick up unwanted energy again and need to ground it out. Knowing what that better state feels like also makes it easier for you to get back to that state at times when you are energetically overwhelmed.

When you've finished your visualization and feel your energy field all clear and clean and shiny, open your eyes and continue with your shower. Revel in the feeling of a squeaky clean energy field!

The shower is a great place to ground out unwanted energy. Creating a regular routine or ritual for clearing your energy field whenever you shower makes a major positive contribution to your health and well-being in body, mind and spirit. It's a good habit for empathic control.

Next, we'll look at using water symbolically, as opposed to physically, to ground out unwanted energy.

We've worked literally with water to clear and ground out unwanted energy; but water can be powerful as a symbol, as well as in its physical form.

We're going to use a visualization combining the symbolic power of water and of Light to help release and ground excess, negative or "stuck" energy.

Guided Visualization For Clearing Negative Energy

Place yourself in a comfortable position sitting or reclining, with arms and legs uncrossed. (If you "drop off" or go to sleep when meditating, probably better for you to do this sitting up.) Adjust your position until comfortable, so your body will not distract you during the visualization. (Wiggle if needed to get comfortable.) If you're seated, it's good to place your feet with soles flat on the floor.

Close your eyes now, and start to relax.

Feel the relaxation sinking slowly and deeply into every single part of your body. Every muscle, every bone, every nerve, is heavy, so very heavy and so very, very relaxed. Become aware of your breath as you breathe in and breathe out, breathe in and breathe out; and, with every breath, you become more and more relaxed.

Picture yourself in a green, green forest. Look around you, seeing the beauty of the wood. The trees are tall and strong and green, and here and there, a ray of sunshine beams down into the deep green shade of the wood. The air is crisp and clean and smells wonderful as you breathe in and breathe out, breathe in and breathe out. The forest is still and quiet, except for the little sounds of a living wood, the sounds of birds and small creatures and green things growing. The ground is firm and solid beneath your feet. You are moving slowly through the woods and you feel wonderful in this green, safe and beautiful place.

After a few moments, you come to a clearing. In the clearing is a beautiful secluded woodland pool, nestled in the heart of the wood. Coming closer to the pool, you see that it is full of light, a beautiful fluid light that combines all of the colors imaginable. It glistens and shines, rippling and gurgling like water, but shining with light.

You sit down on the rocks at the side of the pool; removing one of your shoes. You dip one foot gently into the light. It feels wonderful; warm enough to be healing and comforting, yet cool enough to refresh you as well. It feels so wonderful that you decide to take a dip in the pool.

You wade into the pool of Light, and, as the Light covers each part of your body, it becomes energized and relaxed all at once, and bursting with health. You feel the Light cover your feet, your ankles, your calves, your thighs; your hips, your back, your stomach, your chest; your hands, your forearms, your upper arms; your neck, your scalp, your face. Your entire body is healthy and relaxed in the Light. Take some time to enjoy this wonderful feeling of relaxation and health and Light.

As you move to the far end of the pool, you see a light fall there, a shining cascade of Light splashing into the pool, renewing and refreshing it. The play of the colors in the light fall is beautiful, and the sound of it splashing into the pool is soothing and refreshing.

You move forward into the light fall and the Light is falling on all sides of you, in front of you, in back of you, on the left of you and the right of you, and even pouring through you, and through your energy field. Any excess, negative, or "stuck" energy; any dysfunction; any illness or injury; and anything that interferes with you being your best and brightest self is washed out of you and away from you, clean away from you. You are filled and surrounded by the soothing, healing, transforming Light.

Be aware of how your body and your energy field feel, of the difference between how it feels now and how it felt when you were carrying unwanted energy. Take a moment and enjoy how it feels to be free of that energy.

When you feel the time is right, when you feel that you have cleared all of the unwanted energy that you are ready, willing and able to do at the present time, and you feel cleared, cleansed and healed, you can move out from under the beautiful light fall. You feel wonderful as you come out of the pool and everything that limited you is gone, washed away by the Light.

And now it's time to come back. Begin to become more aware, more aware of your breathing, more aware of your body in the chair, more aware of the room around you and slowly, when you are ready, slowly open your eyes.

This is a very pleasant, powerful and useful meditation, which uses the symbolism of water and light for clearing excess, negative or "stuck" energy, but also for other things. It works well with the mind- body connection to clear chronic pain or illness, and improve the body's ability to heal itself. It can be used to clear negative or dysfunctional beliefs. It can decrease stress and anxiety; and it feels good whenever you do it (which makes it worth doing often just for the sake of that feeling alone.)

Please remember the difference in feeling between carrying that unwanted energy and being free of the weight of it. Knowing that helps you to know when you need to do something to maintain your personal energetic space, and also motivates you to do something about it.

Next up, we're going to take a look at a technique that interacts directly with your energy system.

There are lots of different people in this world, all with their own unique needs and tastes. This is true of empaths, too. There's no one method of grounding out energy that's best for everyone. Because of this, I've tried to offer you choices. We've looked at quite few ways of clearing, releasing and grounded out unwanted energy in this chapter, and I'm hoping you've found one or more methods here that suit your personal preferences.

In the spirit of completeness, I'd like to close this chapter out with one more useful technique.

In New Age circles, there's a method of dealing with release called "Emotional Freedom Technique" (E.F.T., for short) that's excellent for grounding. Originally designed to help people to clear negative or dysfunctional beliefs and feelings (including phobias and post traumatic stress disorders), it's also great for to releasing, clearing and grounding out unwanted energy, especially the kind of energy that I refer to as "old luggage". (Energy that you have carried around for so long that you've forgotten that you're carrying it, and what it feels like to be without it.) E. F.T. is very effective, easy to learn, and quick and simple to do (taking only a minute or less per round). The technique combines repeating a series of personal affirmations, with gently tapping on points on your body. These points correspond to points in the channels that your energy flows through. E.F.T.'s said to unblock blocked energy, allowing your energy to flow freely again.

It's also great for helping you to ground that unwanted energy out.

There's not enough room in this book to fully explain Emotional Freedom Technique, and all that it can do for you as an empath. E.F.T. is easy to find online, and I wanted you to know about it as another great way of dealing with unwanted energy. Check it out for another powerful tool in your energetic tool kit.

We've finally reached the end of the chapter on ways of grounding out excess, negative or "stuck" energy.

We've gone through the four elements; through earth and air and fire and water. We've worked with mental techniques and physical ones. We've visualized and bounced and washed our hands. We've seen that there are lots and lots of ways of clearing out unwanted energy- more ways that any one person has reason to use.

So there's no good reason, knowing all of this, that any of us has to walk around bent double under the weight of a ton of unwanted energy.

I hope that you've tried as many techniques as possible yourself. I also hope that you have found which ones work the best to meet your own individual and personal needs and tastes. All of them will probably work well for you. Because you're a unique and special person, there will be ones that will fit as if they were made for you. Those are the ones that are most effective for you. Keep all of these techniques in your toolkit, but trot your favorites out on a regular basis in order to keep your energetic field bright, shiny and squeaky clean;

Be aware of how your body and your energetic field feel at any time, so that you know when you need to ground out any excess, negative or "stuck" energy, and remember to ground that energy, both as part of a regular routine, and on an "as needed" basis, to keep your own energy in good shape.

In the next chapter, we'll be talking about your own energy, and how to keep it positive and resistant to invasions by more negative vibes.

Ten
Keeping Your Energy Positive

We've talked about shielding, and how to adjust your shields. We've talked about ways to manage the amount of energy you take in from others. We've talked about ways to ground out unwanted energy.

There's one more step you need to take to thrive, not just survive, as a psychic empath. Besides managing energy intruding on you from other people, you need to know how to manage your own energy. You need to develop a positive emotional energetic set point – a level of positive emotion that you naturally live at, and that you automatically return to when you're temporarily knocked off center.

At the end of the day, it's really not enough to only manage how you interact with other people's energy. To have a great life as an empath, you also need to manage your own personal emotional levels. You need to develop a standard level of positive energy, have a strategy for maintaining this positive energy, and also ways for getting to that positive level (or an even better one, if possible).

Why's this important to us? Well, as you may have heard, Nature abhors a vacuum, and it'll do its very best to fill any open space up with something. This "something" is not necessarily always going to be something that we would like to have.

When you ground out negative energy, you leave an open space behind. This is especially true of old or "stuck"energy - energy that you've carried around with you for a long time. If that space stays empty and open, something will eventually come to fill it, and, since the open space is shaped like negative energy, the odds are good for the refill to be some form of negative energy also …

…Unless, of course, you fill the empty space with something different. And put up (in effect), a metaphysical "No Vacancy" sign.

In many of the exercises in the previous chapter, you may

have noticed that I talked about filling any area that you have cleared with Light. That's the main reason for doing this - in order to prevent negative energy from coming back and reinstating itself, by leaving no open space for it to come into.

Positive personal energy will do the same thing as Light. It can fill those spaces in your energetic field left empty after grounding unwanted energy, and make it much harder for negative energy to come back, or for any new negative energy to move into openings in your energy field.

On top of that, a consistently strong and positive emotional energetic set point tends to offer more resistance to the influx of external energetic vibrations. (If you're smiling, you chase those blues away, right?) Being consistently positive doesn't block your access to the information your empathic talent has to give you; but it does make it much harder for any outside or unwanted energy to move in and set up housekeeping in your own energetic field. When your natural emotional state is grounded, centered and positive, it's much harder for the emotional energy of others to overwhelm you.

Think of a positive emotional energetic set point as being like a large, friendly, calm but firm body guard for your energetic field. Giving you control back over your life again.

This is not just a question of positive thinking (though positive thinking is very effective in general in helping you manifest the kind of life you would like.) Beyond positive thinking, it's more of a practice of keeping your energy levels consistently positive, so that they remain positive without you having to consciously think about it. When your emotional set point automatically defaults to the positive, when you don't even have to think about it for it to happen, that positive energy is constantly on duty to help keep out negative energy that's not in your best interests.

This doesn't mean that, if you're not happy all of the time, you're doing this whole personal energy level thing wrong, and will immediately be overrun with other peoples' invasive energies. No one person, including me, is perfect. Everybody has had a bad hair day or two.

It's more of a question of choosing to hold the most positive vibration that you can at any particular moment. Of building a positive energy habit, so that, if you're knocked off center, you'll automatically return to that positive point as quickly and easily as possible.

Developing that positive set point is the last step to gaining control of your empathic gift. Factors as diverse as nutrition, positive thinking and keeping your commitments to yourself go a long way towards keeping your emotional set point strong and positive.

And that's what you need. To not only be able to control what you take in from other people, but also to keep your personal energy strong and positive.

Luckily, we've got ways to do that just ahead.

The first step of building a state of positive energy is to be aware of what you feel like when you're in a negative one.

Start by finding a quiet place where you will not be distracted. Close your eyes. Now think about something that makes you feel very angry....

Got it? Good.

Now pay attention to your body and your energy field. Where do you feel the anger? In your back? Your jaw? Your stomach? Your forehead? How does anger make your energy field feel?

Noted the tell tale symptoms of anger? Good. Now relax and return to neutral.

Once back to neutral, repeat this with other negative emotions such as anxiety, fear, depression, and jealousy. Note the tell tales for each emotion; and remember to relax and return to neutral between each emotion check, so you feel the differences between the vibrations of the different emotions.

Remember these symptoms. When you feel them in everyday life, that's your signal that you're sliding into a negative state, and need to do something to stop that slide. Ground. Shield. Or do something to turn your emotional state more positive.

Once you've got the negative states down, now go over the positive ones. Close your eyes and think about something that makes you feel calm, positive, and centered, without getting manic, hysterical or giddy. This is the set point level that you're looking to make into a habit; a default setting that you'll return to consistently.

Got your set point? Good.

Pay attention to your body and energy field again. How does being at center feel? Where do you feel this emotion? How does your face feel? Your body? How does it make your energy field feel?

Remember these symptoms too. They're here to help you achieve your emotional set point, and we're going to use them in the next exercise.

We want to find ways to reach that positive set point easily and quickly. One way of doing that is to use the mind - body connection.

Most people think of the mind – body connection as the mind affecting the body. For instance, if you think you're going to get the flu, that belief passes from your mind to your body, having a negative effect on your immune system and making you more likely to get sick. Health comes from a collection of factors, including nutrition, genetics, environment, immunity, and much more besides; but multiple studies have found that attitudes and beliefs are two factors that tip the scales towards good or ill.

Your thoughts can physically affect your body. What most people don't realize is that the mind – body connection works in both directions.

Your body can have an effect upon your thoughts.

Interesting....

Remember those symptoms of different emotional states you collected in the previous exercise. We're going to use them now.

Let's start with depression. Think about something that

makes you feel very sad.

Got that? Good.

Be aware of your body and energy field. How does it feel when you are sad? What is your body doing?

When most people are depressed, they slump or slouch. They hunch their shoulders. Their jaws are tense, and their mouths frowning. Their eyes turn downward, avoiding eye contact. They may clasp their hands tightly together, or shove them deeply into their pockets. Their energy fields feel dim, murky or muddy, like they're shutting off all positive possibilities.

Your results may be different, but you'll probably find that you have at least some of these symptoms.

Now, think about something that makes you feel very calm, positive, centered and in control of your life.

Got it? Good.

Be aware of your body and energy field. How does it feel when you are positive, calm and centered? What's your body doing now?

When most people are positive and centered, they tend to stand more upright. Their shoulders are held back. Their eyes are open and looking around, often shining with interest or joy. They usually make eye contact with people and things. Their jaws are relaxed, and their mouths are smiling. Their hands are relaxed, and usually either by their sides or doing something. Their energy fields feel clear, clean and lively.

Once again, your mileage may vary. You may find you differ from this in how your body and energy field feel in your ideal state. That's fine - just be aware of what this state feels like for you.

And now, we're going to try an experiment...

Keep your body in that positive position. Upright, shoulders back, muscles relaxed, eye contact, mouth smiling....

Now try to think about feeling sad.

Go ahead – try it....

(Hard, isn't it?...)

You're likely finding that it's more challenging to fully

connect with the emotion of "sorrow" than it was for you before. The feeling may feel distant, vague, or somewhat unreal.

So, what's happening here, anyway?

This exercise shows one way the mind - body connection works. Your unconscious mind, which has control over a good deal of metaphysical ability, including the mind-body connection, believes everything you tell it.

When your body adopts the position your unconscious associates with "positive, calm, centered, happy", the unconscious mind believes that things are fine, and goes to work to make this real. This includes keeping your energy field in a positive state (since it believes this is what's happening...)

What's this mean for you and me?

It means that when I notice that I'm starting to get "depression shoulders", I need to do something to pick myself up a little. It means if your energy starts to go in a negative direction (whether due to other people's negativity or your own bad mood), you can boost yourself back in the right direction by standing up straight, throwing your shoulders back and smiling a bit...

It seems like, when your mother told you to "straighten up and fly right", she knew what she was talking about...

We've just used the mind – body connection to change the emotional level of our energy field. That's not the only way to use your body to shift your energy.

Feeling overwhelmed, anxious, angry, or down? Instead of suffering, try this. Take a deep breath, and, keeping your head level, roll your eyes up and look at the ceiling. (Repeat as needed...)

Try it right now. Think of something that brings you down (taxes, your least-favorite co-worker, cleaning out the fridge,...). Notice how that makes you feel - where it hits you in body and energy field...

Breathe deep and look up at the ceiling. Feel the difference? How do you feel now? How does your body feel?

How does your energy field feel?

While not a substitute for Prozac, most people find that, when they do this technique, they feel more positive, centered and able to cope with whatever's happening.

So, how does this work?

When we're feeling stressed or negative, we breathe in shorter, quicker, shallower breaths. Breathing deeply and slowly triggers a mind-body connection saying that "all is well", and actually puts us in a better energetic place. Looking up seems to strengthen this energetic reaction (and when I'm facing major challenges, I find that looking up is valuable for spiritual reasons as well…).

I like to think we're all hardwired with a variety of ways to shift our energy into more positive forms.

This technique is excellent vibrational emergency first aid. It's quick, easy, can be done almost anywhere, and does not require any special equipment. Using this method, when you notice that you're beginning to develop "sorrow shoulder" or a touch of "anger jaw" you can adjust your emotional level upwards in 30 seconds or less. It can also make a significant contribution as part of a program of long-term energetic maintenance, but it really shines as an "on the spot" emergency technique.

Just one final precaution - do not do this in front of your bossy aunt Margaret, your unpleasant supervisor or any other person making a present to you of their negative energy. People who are bringers of stress will surely take this technique the wrong way, and that is definitely the path to an additional download of negative energy …

So remember- when times get tough, just breathe deep and look up.

We've worked in different ways with your body for a positive effect on your emotional energetic field. Let's go a different way, and use your mind to improve your energy instead. What if you could use your thoughts to easily shift your emotional vibration upwards? Feel better just by thinking?

You can. And here's how.

One way to think about emotions is as a progressive scale like the one in this chapter, with the most negative emotions at the bottom of the scale and the most positive ones at the top. The higher an emotion falls on the scale, the higher the vibration associated with it.

The Emotional Scale

12) Empowerment, freedom, appreciation, joy, love

11) Passion, enthusiasm

10) Happiness, positive anticipation, delight

9) Optimism, gratitude, belief

8) Hope, faith, contentment

7) Frustration, irritation, impatience

6) Pessimism, overwhelmed, apathy

5) Disappointment, doubt

4) Worry, anxiety

3) Anger, hatred, jealousy

2) Unworthiness, insecurity, guilt

1) Sorrow, depression, fear, powerlessness

We think of emotions as "positive" or "negative". If, however, you look at them as part of a scale, you'll find that they're more positive or less so when compared to other emotions. For example, we see "anger" as negative, but, if you're coming from deep depression, anger is less negative and a step up. At that point, anger gives you strength to move out of despair's immobility and upwards. You won't want to stay in anger indefinitely, but if you're coming up from depression, it can be a step in the right direction.

Why does that matter to us as empaths? Because we can use this scale, or one like it, to work up and out of more negative emotions and to reach more positive ones. It's a great tool for getting to our positive emotional energetic set point, and for keeping ourselves there.

We do this by taking four steps

- Identifying the emotional level that we are on now;
- Looking at the next step up from this level;
- Finding a thought about what's happening that puts us on that next level up;
- Repeating the first three steps, if we can, to move as far up the emotional scale as possible.

For example, what if your partner promised to take you out to a special dinner, and, at the very last minute, had to cancel on you?

- First, you may feel disappointed.
  (5) "Rats. No dinner out."
- Looking at the scale, you can move your thoughts from this to pessimism
  (6) "We never get to go out to eat."
- From there, go up to irritation.
  (7) "Can't believe he's working late again"

So far, these are all negative emotions, although gradually improving ones. But with the next step, faith:

- *(8) "We haven't gotten out to eat so far, but I believe it'll happen by the end of the week",*

we're into the positive emotions. We can keep working upwards just by using the scale again.

At first, this may sound like just an exercise on paper. It's not, and, when you try it out, you'll see this for yourself. My experience is that, by looking for a thought that we can accept (one slightly better than what we're currently holding), we can change our beliefs and change our feelings about what is happening around us. Doing this, we also change our emotional energetic vibration, and the kind of things we attract into our lives. (Since like calls to like, more positive emotional energy attracts more positive people, things and experiences.)

This works because, when you are in a situation and chose a better thought about it, part of creating that thought is feeling the emotion itself. That improves the level of your emotional vibration.

You chose a better thought. You create a better feeling. You attract a better reality.

When using the emotional scale to move up to more positive levels, some people rise several levels in a session. Some can only move up one step. How much change you experience depends on who you are and on the situation at the time. Whether you rise from bottom to top of scale, or only one level, the scale works best if you go one level at a time. Going through levels one by one lets you feel the transitions and integrates them; but trying to jump multiple levels at once can leave you in a thought/ emotion that feels unreal and therefore doesn't shift your energy.

Depending on what's happening, you may only be able to move up a single level. You may be able to move up to the top of the scale in gradual steps. Either of these or anything in between is absolutely fine, because our basic objective is to get your emotional energy to the best level possible at the moment. Good enough really is good enough. And even a slight improvement in your emotional energy can improve your world.

Once you're used to working with the emotional scale, moving up a level only takes a few seconds, and the results are certainly worth it. This means that, at any time, you can choose to change your mood, to be at an emotional level that feels better to you, and to attract a better reality, regardless of the one you're currently in.

And that's priceless.

We've looked at improving your energetic levels, by choosing thoughts that move you to a better emotional state. What if you were choosing that kind of thought on a regular basis?

The practice of positive thinking has been on the books for a very long time. It has a proven track record of improving peoples' quality of life, both psychologically and energetically.

Contrary to what some people believe, positive thinking is not about denying reality, lying to yourself, or playing Pollyanna. It's about choosing the best belief possible for you at any time, and letting that best thought positively shape reality around you.

Does that seem just a bit simplistic? Well, it's not quite as silly as it may look.

Many medical studies have found that stress isn't actually caused by things that happen to us. Rather, it's caused by beliefs we form about what happens to us. That's how two people can have the same experience, and one freaks out, while the other stays cool as a cucumber.

For instance, a torrential downpour breaks out. One person thinks "This always happens to me!". The other one thinks "Drat! Wish I had an umbrella!"

The umbrella guy may have squelchy socks until he gets

home and changes them, but the rain will pass and his day will get better, because he's focused on better things. The guy who took the storm personally, however, will be carrying his bad mood and feeling of powerlessness around with him long after the storm has ended. Energetically, umbrella guy's energetic field will stay strong and intact. Mr. Personal will pick up any further bad energy that drifts by, because like calls to like.

That's one reason why you want to think the most positive thought you can at any moment.

Psychologically, whether in a positive or negative mindset, you tend to look for evidence in life that supports the beliefs that created your mindset in the first place. Metaphysically, you'll also tend to attract those kinds of things....

The negative mindset looks for proof that you're a victim; that the world is a frightening, unfair place; and that nothing you do makes any difference. The positive mindset looks for opportunities to learn, grow and succeed, friendly people, and evidence that the world is wonderful. And each mindset creates the world it believes in, both by selecting for it, and attracting it.

Now, which person do you think is going to create a more pleasant world to live in?

From a psychological and physiological standpoint, a habitually negative mindset creates an impaired immune system, poor judgment, and victim mentality. A positive mindset supports better health, flexibility and resilience, and the adaptability to make the most of any situation.

From a metaphysical standpoint, a negative mindset depletes your energy, leaving you open to being overrun by external energy. It attracts more negative energy and experiences to you.

On the other hand, the positive mindset creates a strong energy field that helps to protect you from incursion by external energy. It also attracts more positive energy, experiences and people into your world.

From either standpoint, positive thinking does a body

good....

So, can you wave a magick wand and suddenly have only good thoughts all the time? Well, I can't. Even though I'm fairly positive, I still have cranky, anxious and down times. Sometimes, cranky, anxious or down may be the best choice available to you.

Eventually, you want to get to the point where you have the most positive energetic emotional level possible in any moment. There are some things you can do to make that happen.

First, be aware of how you're feeling. Listen to your body. Listen to your thoughts. Listen to your heart. Many of us slide into emotional bad spaces because we're either out of touch with our feelings, or else in major denial about them because they are uncomfortable to us. This can make us miss the signs that we're heading into negative energy. We can end up in much worse emotional states if we don't head problems off while they're still small.

So pay attention to how you're feeling. Check in with your psyche over the day. Watch for cues from your body we identified in the mind-body exercises. Ask yourself "How do I feel about this?'

And when you find you're going downhill, ask yourself questions. But make sure that they're good questions. ..
Like:

- "How can I make this work?"
- "What's good about this situation?"
- "What thought would feel better right now?"
- "What can I do to raise my emotional level?
- "Is this important enough to make myself feel bad about?"

And so forth. The goal here is to find a way of thinking about your situation that feels better than the thought that is dragging you down. And when you find that thought, to latch onto it and see if you can find an even better thought than that.

Making a habit of consciously choosing the best possible thought in stress-free times is like training like an athlete. If you always head towards a positive thought, that will be your default when times get challenging and negative chaotic energy swirls around you.

You'll strengthen your energy field and increase your resistance to outside incursion using positive energy. Your shields will strengthen when energy around you becomes overwhelming. You'll remember to use energetic management techniques, because your positive energy and stronger shields already give you enough breathing space to think. You'll ground out stray overwhelming or negative energy that breaks through your protections. And you'll get the information your empathy has gathered for you, without getting knocked out of kilter in the process.

So remember to think the good thought when you can. It puts you in the driver's seat.

One technique related to positive thinking is using a focus to regain your positive emotional level. When you're feeling negative (due to someone else's energy, or energy you've created yourself) or, caught in a downwards spiral, a classic remedy is focusing on things more positive than the negative ones that brought you down in the first place. In other words, counting your blessings.

Unfortunately, when you're depressed, it can be hard to come up with things that make you feel happy, let alone focus on them.

You and I need to plan ahead, right?...

Build yourself a safety net. Pick a time when you're well grounded and centered energetically - a time when you're calm, collected and positive. Pick a time when you feel good, when the positive side of the Force is with you.

This is the time to take a moment or two, and brainstorm a list of things that make you happy when you think about them. Kittens and puppies. Chocolate. Your favorite music. A surprise gift from a friend. Or whatsoever floats your personal boat.

The things on your list should be things that make you feel happy just by thinking about them. If, with an item, you get a "but - I - don't - have - this - right - now - and - that - makes - me – feel – sad..." feeling, it does not belong on this particular list (although it may belong on a list of goals for another day.)

Next, write your list down. Write it on something durable and noticeable. Make multiple copies, if you're so moved. Put your list where you'll see it every day; where you'll remember it and find it easily when things are challenging and you need it. In your day planner. Taped up beside your bathroom mirror. Stuck to the dashboard of your car. Any place you like where it's clearly visible, accessible, and doesn't embarrass you.

Why? Because, when times get tough and negative energy invades your field, thinking of things that make you happy will make it far easier for you to turn things around and raise your energetic levels back up again; but, if you've got the blues, it's hard to remember the positive things that can lift you back up. Written lists remind you to think more positively so you can turn things around, and the things on the lists give you a boost in the right direction. That reminder and that boost may be all you need to get your energy headed back in the right direction.

Are you having a good day now? Then now might be a good time to sit down and start a list of the things that make you smile...

Sometimes, you get an overwhelming blast of negative emotion from out of nowhere. Sometimes it sneaks up on you, like a villain in a bad horror movie. You'll find yourself feeling down, or blue, or frustrated, or overwhelmed; and you won't seem to be able to break free of it.

At times like these, the very best thing you can do for yourself is ask yourself the master question-

"Is this my energy or is it someone else's...?"

This is an important question so let me repeat it ...

"Is this my energy or is it someone else's...?"

This question is an all around useful tool for any psychic empath. It lets you take a moment, step back from what seems to be causing your problems (but may not be), and get calm and centered (perhaps by breathing deeply and looking up). By asking this very simple question, you can gain enormous insight into what's really happening to you energetically. It's surprising how easily the information usually comes to you if you take the time to ask.

Once you know the answer, you'll know whether you need to take steps to deal with external energy, or work on improving energy you're creating for yourself. You'll know whether to strengthen or adjust your shields. You'll know whether to use techniques to manage external energy, and whether leaving the area will help you. You'll know whether you need to ground out energy, and whether you should start working your way up the emotional scale. You can start doing what you need to do to return your energy levels to a more positive state.

Of all of the tools, techniques and information in this book, this simple question is the most important one. Knowing the difference between your own energy and that of other folks puts you back in control of your life.

In short, while an empath needs techniques and skills to control how much energy she takes in from other people, protect from energetic overwhelm, and deal with unwanted energy, she also needs to remember to keep her own energy clean, clear and positive. A positive energy field is a stronger energy field. It makes it easier to keep out energy that you don't want, or that doesn't belong to you. A positive set point makes it easier to maintain a positive energy field, by building a habit of positive energy. And a positive attitude makes it easier to maintain a positive set point.

Besides, being happy is more fun. Not only more fun, but also good for the psychic empath as well. Think about it - how often do the concepts of "more fun" and "good for you" go together like that for you?

So, why not take advantage of that? Do the thing you know is good for you, and smile all the time you're doing it.

Make a habit of positive energy.

Eleven
Sorting Out Energy

We've been through ways to work with unwanted energy; but which method do you need to use when? When facing challenging energy, you may want to evaluate the energy you're receiving empathically, and look at what it's doing to you or for you.

What kind of energy are you experiencing?

If it's negative emotional energy
- Is it serving a functional purpose for you? (ex: The frustration that makes you finally look for another, less negative job.)
- Is it emotionally appropriate to the situation? (ex: Sorrow at the death of someone you care for.)
- Is it alerting you to a problem you need to deal with? (ex: Anxiety or stress that makes you aware of a health problem.)
- Does it have something to tell you?

If it's excess energy
- Is it something you're experiencing as part of a period of high activity (such as the last stages of planning for a wedding?)
- Are you having fun with it? (Sometimes, you can get absolutely giddy from the good vibes of people having fun around you. If it's not unsafe, such energy is enjoyable for a limited amount of time.)
- Are you healthy? Have you had enough sleep? (Sometimes being in pain, sick or sleep deprived can drain you and decrease the amount of energy you can tolerate, leading to a feeling of excess energy.)

If it's overwhelming energy:

- How many issues are you dealing with currently? (Sometimes energetic overload comes from a normal amount of empathic energy piled on top of a large amount of responsibilities or concerns.)
- Have you had enough sleep? Are you in good health? (As noted in excessive energy, being short of sleep or coming down with something can decrease your energetic tolerance, making normal energy feel overwhelming.)

There are times in your life when these kinds of energy may be an appropriate or even a functional response to your situation. It's good to figure out whether you have an uncomfortable situation (needing techniques to manage energy appropriately) or an actual problem (which may require releasing the energy altogether.)

Once you know this, you'll know whether you need to work in the physical plane (doing things such as getting more sleep, or delegating tasks so your workload is workable) so you have the personal resources you need to deal with energy. You'll know if you need to better manage energy (by increasing the strength of your shields, or doing an energetic "chop"). You'll know if you're through with this energy, and if you should release it by grounding it out. And you'll be able to take the steps you need to make your world a better place for you.

Twelve
The Projective Empath

We've learned about the gift of empathy, and run through skills and techniques to give you control over your gift. Let's talk about a variation of psychic empathy.

All psychic empaths are receptive empaths. They receive emotional energy from people around them, and gain information from it that can be used for their benefit, and that of the world.

Some psychic empaths are also projective / radiant empaths. I don't know how many receptive empaths are also projective, but many of them can project emotional vibrations outwards, as well as receive them from outside of themselves.

A projective empath can project emotional vibrations beyond his own energetic field into the world around him. These vibrations can be perceived by other people, both empaths and non - empaths. A projective empath cannot **force** people to feel things, but he can create a space that encourages and supports that emotion. It's a question of a gentle influence, rather than massive control.

How's that useful to you? Well, if you're a projective / radiant empath, you can:

- Project competence in your work situation;
- Project friendliness when meeting people;
- Project kind firmness when disciplining children;
- Project reliability on a job interview;
- Project calm if someone is upset or hysterical;
- Project honesty and responsiveness when trying to reach an agreement with others;
- Project confidence when teaching or speaking in front of people;
- Project reasonableness when making a proposal;
- Project care and concern if you're trying to help someone who's upset;

- Project that you are "not prey" if you must walk through a hazardous area. (Please don't count on this projection alone. The best way to avoid danger is to *avoid danger;* but if you find yourself in such a situation, this ability can help keep you safe.);

And so forth...

Radiant empaths don't just project positive feelings, though. If they don't have energetic control, lose it due to negativity, or don't choose to maintain control over their empathy, they can also project negative emotions:

- When a radiant empath is mad, everyone had best get out of his way. A cold word from an angry projective can sound like it's screamed at the top of his voice (especially if the recipient is an empath..).
- An anxious projective empath can raise the blood pressure in every person around him.
- And there is no wet blanket as soggy as a depressive radiant empath. If a projective empath is seriously blue, and not controlling his gift, he can spoil a party just by walking into the room.

For this reason, it's even more important for a radiant empath to control his emotional level (as discussed in chapter 10), control his empathic gift, or both.

Besides that, it's difficult (while not impossible) to project an emotion you're not actually feeling (though, by choosing to project an emotion, you may increase how much you feel it yourself). For this reason, being a radiant empath is no help with deceiving people. It does help, however, with making connections with other people, supporting them in their roles and challenges, and helping yourself in life.

If you've been working on getting better control of your receptive empathy, you may want to see if you are a radiant or projective empath as well.

Are You a Projective/Radiant Empath?...

1) Do people tend to avoid "messing with" you?
2) Are you very persuasive?
3) Do friends with problems find they feel better after talking to you about them?
4) Are you the life of the party?
5) Do people feel safe and secure around you?
6) Are you good at selling things?
7) Are you good at selling people on things?
8) Could "When momma's not happy, nobody's happy..." apply to you?
9) Can you talk your way out of anything?
10) Are you really good at getting people to compromise or see the other side of things?

How'd you do? Like the previous psychic empathy quiz, you could have any of these characteristics for other reasons besides psychic ability, but the more of them you have, the more likely it is that you are a radiant empath.

So let's talk about how to work with that ability.

How does a radiant empath energetically "project" an emotional vibration?

You start by feeling the emotion yourself.

Close your eyes. Get in touch with the feeling you want to share with the world around you. Listen to the emotion and how it feels. Listen to how your body experiences that emotion.

What does it feel like to feel this feeling?

- How does it feel to you emotionally? Is it warm, or cheerful, or exciting, or tense? What are the basic qualities of this feeling?
- What does your body do when you feel this way? Do you relax or perk up?
- What are the physical sensations you associate with this emotion?
- How does it feel in various parts of your body? Your face? Your jaw? Your neck? Your shoulders? Your back? Your stomach?
- What memory from your past might help you make a closer connection with this feeling?

Finding ways of experiencing this feeling more closely or intensely make it easier to project.

If you've found the physical qualities that go with this feeling, and you're not presently engaged in these activities, changing your body language or "acting as if" you were feeling them can actually strengthen the emotion within you.

- Smile widely, if you're trying to project joy.
- Tense your shoulders, if you're trying to project "don't mess with me".
- Relax jaw, neck, shoulders and back, if you're trying to project calm;

And so on…

It's not just a question of body language sending a non-verbal message of emotion to the person that you're trying to reach. More that, when your body takes the position associated with an emotion, you'll feel it more deeply or intensely, and therefore be more able to project it.

First, you put the sunshine in your own heart…

Once you're fully feeling the emotion yourself, focus on how the emotional energy feels inside of you. I usually feel it glowing around my abdomen and solar plexus like a bright and shining little sun. You may experience it differently than I do. That's perfectly fine – whatever image or connection works for you is good.

Got that connection yet? Good for you.

Now you're going to feel it getting larger. You're going to "push" the energy out, first to the edge of, and then beyond the borders of your personal energy field and shields.

Some of us may "see" that ball of energy getting larger and larger until it finally extends outside of the body. Some of us feel a non-physical "push" to get the energy out there. (Some people may even find themselves physically "pushing" the air at first). And some of us may "just know" it's happening as we focus on it …

This may seem involved at first. As you practice it, you'll find it gets easier and easier until it's effortless and almost instantaneous. Indeed, some empaths may find they have a natural skill for this, or that they've already been unconsciously doing this all along. Practice also makes it easier to maintain projected energy for longer periods of time with less effort.

Remember to keep the intention as you project emotional energy that your shields keep you protected from any negative or overwhelming energy around you.

Then let your light shine…

One major advantage of being a receptive empath is that it helps you to connect with people around you. It helps you understand where they're coming from, and that helps you communicate in a way that speaks to where they're really at, as opposed to only what they're saying.

If you're a projective empath, you can be even better at connecting with people around you. You can energetically connect with people on an emotional level. Speak with them with your spirit, as well as your mouth. "Hear" them with your heart.

Much of our communication is not only through speech, but also through non-verbal body language. We don't just listen when we communicate. We pick up things using our other senses as well. And, here we get to move beyond the basic five.

I'm talking here about moving beyond non-verbal communication, to the level of subtle energetic vibrations. It's interesting to note that, while it takes a psychic empath to pick up regular emotional vibrations, emotions projected energetically by a radiant empath are picked up by empaths and non-empaths alike (although not everyone consciously notices this).

Once you have more experience projecting emotional vibrations, and don't need to work as hard to do this, you may want to start making it part of your regular communication.

- When you praise your child, send her the feeling of how proud you are of her, as well as telling her so.
- When you're trying to inspire a group to work together effectively, send a feeling of confidence as you tell them you know that they can do it.
- When you're with someone overwhelmed, upset and hysterical, send a feeling of quiet strength and calm as you pat them on the back and tell them that things are going to be o.k.
- When you give constructive criticism, project a feeling of compassion and support, to make it easier for the person to hear and use the feedback without feeling defensive and resistive.
- When you're with someone you love, send that love

as well as say it.

Say it and send it, and they'll hear you much better.

When speaking with both voice and energy, the message you give is deeper, stronger, and more likely to be taken in and believed or acted on.

You don't always have to "say it", to send a message. Projected emotional energy alone can reach people with profound effects, even when not accompanied by words.

- Sending loving energy to your partner or children can improve their mood and their health.
- Putting out "don't mess with me / I am not prey" energy decreases chances that you'll be attacked.
- Emotional vibes sent to people who do not speak your language often creates a connection although you cannot speak directly.
- Emotional energy sent to people who are non-verbal due to injury, illness or developmental disability can create a connection on an energetic level, leading to better interactions and co-operation.
- Radiant empathic energy can even be perceived by animals, both ones who know you and ones new to you. Projecting calm can help to sooth a skittish horse or injured cat. Projecting confidence can make you the alpha in your dog's life, making training easier.

While there are always exceptions to the rule in any of the above circumstances, as a whole, projected empathic vibrations can function effectively independently of spoken language, and can help make your world a better place in a wide variety of ways. Projected emotional vibrations are another way you can use your empathic skills to improve your world, by making better connections with the people around you.

We've talked about using empathic projection to make a better connection with people around you. What about using it to improve mutual understanding and communication in other ways? Let's talk about helping people resolve their differences.

You may recall that, as a receptive empath, you have an edge at times where people are disagreeing because you're directly in touch with how they're feeling. You can tell:

- when people aren't satisfied, even if they say they are;
- when people are being deceptive;
- when people are ready to blow up and may need a break;
- when people are honestly doing what they believe is the best that they can;

And other useful information that can help you reach an agreement that will last, as opposed to a patched together fantasy that falls apart of its' own weight the first time that it's stressed.

Let's try adding projective empathy to the mix and see what happens.

When you add projective emotional vibrations to a situation where you're trying to resolve conflict, you can:

- Project honesty and fairness, and decrease paranoia and defensiveness in the group.
- Project compassion, and inspire better give and take in those around you.
- Project calm, and let discussions be less acrimonious.
- Project respect, and watch people become more mutually respectful, (some of them because they'll be embarrassed

to act otherwise.)

- Project strength and competence, and be more easily able to lead and steer the meeting towards something fair to everyone, with far less resistance from individual participants.

The combination of inside information you obtain through receptive empathy, and an atmosphere generated using projective empathy that supports general co-operation can help you to:

- ensure that everyone in conflict feels truly heard;
- separate actual issues from created obstacles or overreactions;
- understand what each party truly wants and needs;
- know when people have something to contribute, but aren't speaking up;
- find common ground to help participants better understand each other;
- translate needs into things in common so people move towards working with each other;
- help people understand that together we can create a solution where everyone wins;
- create a better, more co-operative structure for conflict resolution, where people work together to reach a "win-win" solution;
- generate that "win-win" solution - one based on mutual agreements not grudging concessions, that is more likely to last for the long haul.

This is complex but organic conflict management you can use to reach agreements throughout your life, whether in a high powered corporate meeting or in reaching an agreement with your child. It's done by "listening" with your empathic gift as well as your ears, and adding energy to make it easier for folks to see each others' sides of situations and the benefits of working together to solve the problem, rather than continue in conflict.

At its best, you may be shifting from one emotion to another as needed. This is tricky at first, but becomes easier with experience; and the results you get, which are good for everyone involved, are more than worth learning to juggle energy....

Together, receptive and projective empathy are a powerful combination for resolving conflict. It helps you to better understand others, and be better understood by others yourself.

By now, I'm sure you can see there are lots of nifty uses for projective empathy. Let me lay another one on you now. It's great for using in the performing arts. Singing. Dancing. Acting. Public Speaking. (Even mime...)

(Just think about it a moment...)

It can also help in different types of teaching, lecturing, public demonstrations and other presentations to people.

Just as combining projective empathy with speaking creates a deeper, more genuine message, and silently using projective empathy creates a clear message without the use of words, so combining radiant empathy with performing arts (whether vocal performances or silent ones) creates a deeper, richer, more genuine experience for both audience and performer.

This performance technique takes practice to work well for you and your audience. Just as a singer practices both the words of a song and the act of singing itself, so you'll need to practice projecting the emotional vibration you want in duet with your performance.

It's good to give some thought to what emotion or combination of emotions you want to project while performing. You may choose the vibration based on the nature and tone of your performance, or you might choose your emotion based on the experience of performing itself. Some of the most wonderful experiences I've had as a performer involved projecting "I love you, and I love performing for you" to my audience, and feeling the energy bounce back from them and return to me, magnified by the feelings of the people watching the show.

First, practice projecting the emotion, as discussed earlier in this chapter. Then practice combining this with your actual act until it's a matter of habit. Once you can do it automatically, without even thinking about it, you're ready to actually incorporate projective empathy in your performance.

When performing for an audience and empathically projecting emotional energy as a part of the performance, you may find that the audience catches that vibration and returns it to you, magnified in intensity or transformed into something different altogether. A good empathic performance can end up turning into a feedback loop, with vibrations passing back and forth between audience and entertainer for the length of the show. This can be a heady experience for the empathic performer. If this type of empathic feedback happens, the audience usually does it unconsciously, but occasionally this response is a conscious empathic response to what you're doing.

What's more, in addition to the emotional energy you're projecting to your audience and feedback from that energy, you'll often get incoming energetic input from the audience as well. Being prepared for energy coming at you means you can expect it, enjoy positive vibrations and throw off anything less than supportive, instead of being overwhelmed by it.

So, with projective energy, audience energetic feedback to the original projection, and independent energy generated in response to the performance itself, an empathic performance can be a work of art on multiple levels.

Now you know how to project emotional energy empathically, and you've already got some basic ideas about what you can do with it. What's one of the best things you can use it for? Making an emotionally safe space for people.

Most people are afraid to fail, because failure is punished so vigorously and so cruelly. Because of this, most are afraid to try new things and move outside of their comfort zones, because some failure is likely as part of the learning process.

This fear makes for sad and lousy lives. People who are afraid to love, or who leave relationships at the first sign of trouble, because failure is too painful. People who abandon their dreams, because they might fail trying to get them. People who live mediocre existences, because not trying keeps them safe from possible failure.

Here's one place that you can make a difference.

Something you can project is belief and acceptance. Belief that any person can do great things. Acceptance that there will be some mistakes and false starts along the way, because this is part of the learning process. The feeling that around you is a safe space to experiment, learn and grow.

Creating an atmosphere of acceptance can help people have better lives by making it safe for them to fail so that it's also safe to succeed, achieve, learn and grow. As they experience that acceptance within your energy field, they'll gradually learn to take that new courage into the world beyond what you've built for them, learning to learn and grow independently without being stopped by fear.

You can help them make their dreams come true. And that's a beautiful thing.

We've come to the end of the chapter on the radiant or projective side of psychic empathy. We've determined if you have the skill, and talked about how to energetically project emotional vibrations. We've looked at some of the ways this type of empathy can be used to help you and people around you:

- To better understand people.
- To reassure animals.
- To communicate without words.

- To create a closer connection with another person;
- To resolve conflict.
- To make it easier for people to work and play nicely together.
- To help people understand each other.
- To translate people's concerns so that they can see their common ground.
- To encourage people to better co-operate and work together.
- To enrich public speaking and the performing arts.
- To create a safe space for people to learn and grow.
- To help people overcome fear of failure.
- To help people pursue their Life Missions and dreams by creating a safe space to experiment in.

There are many other applications for projective empathy. (Just stop and think for a moment, - I'm sure that, at this point, you can come up with some ideas on your own).

As I said at the start of this chapter, it's important to remember that a projective empath cannot **force** another person to feel a certain way, however the radiant empath can create a field of energy that encourages peoples' emotions to turn in that particular direction. Psychic empathy is persuasive, as opposed to coercive. Within those limitations though, a skill with radiant or projective empathy can be a strong and useful ability - one that's well worth taking the effort to learn to use.

So don't hide your light under a bushel. Let your light shine...

Thirteen
Better Living Through Psychic Empathy

We've covered a great deal of ground already.

- We've looked at how to tell if you're a psychic empath, and what that can mean to you.
- We've looked at ethical behavior for psychics of all sorts, including empaths.
- We've covered negative, overwhelming, and "stuck" energy, and the destructive effects these types of energy can have on you.
- We've looked at energetic shields for keeping your own energy separate from other people's; and at other techniques for controlling how much energy you're exposed to from the world around you.
- We've talked about different ways for you to get rid of unwanted energy by grounding it out in the earth and in other elements.
- We've talked about ways to keep your own energy positive, both to resist negative energy created by others, and to avoid contributing your home-made negativity to problem energy you must deal with.
- We've talked about projective or radiant psychic empathy – how to do it, and ways to use it.

We've talked about controlling your psychic gift, rather than letting it control you. That's what you need to know to make your gift a true gift to you and the world around you, rather than a burden.

We've looked at a lot of things. We've still got much more to go; because, once you get a handle on your gift of empathy, that's when it gets useful. (And fun, too...)

In this chapter, we're going to talk about things you need

to know about how to use your empathic gift.

Once you have control of your empathy (rather than it controlling you), there are a lot of good uses for it.

First, it gives you insight into people around you.

What's that good for? For starters....

- To better understand people you encounter in life;
- To help you make wiser, more informed choices;
- To support your personal safety;
- To know when people need extra attention;
- To help folks to reach understanding with each other and create common ground between them;
- To nurture the people you love and care for;
- To know who can be trusted and who cannot;
- To overcome misunderstandings, big and small;
- To know when your kids are up to mischief;
- In negotiations, to reach compromises agreeable to all parties more easily;
- To help people feel more comfortable around you;
- To be more aware of dangerous situations;
- It's also great for the performing arts- you can sing with your spirit as well as your mouth;
- To make your corner of the cosmos a kinder, better place to be;

And lots of other fun and useful skills, mostly related to connecting with people in the world around you...

When you know where people are really coming from, it makes it easier to successfully interact with them. It gives you an edge over people around you.

As an empath, the skills that give you control of your gift makes both your personal world, and the world around you a warmer, kinder, more beautiful place.

Psychic empathy can give you more insight into people around you. This can keep you safer.

Here's how it works. When a person is deceptive, dishonest, or sly, his energetic vibrations (reflecting his real emotions) don't match the emotion he's portraying. For an empath, that feels like a vague feeling of unease, often in neck or back tension; or butterflies in the stomach.

Sometimes, this discrepancy is due to innocent reasons. Maybe your best friend is planning a surprise party. Maybe your mom really dislikes the guy that you're dating, but is too wise or polite to say so.

Sometimes, it's just a heads-up for something small. When you ask your child what he's doing and he answers casually "...nothing...". When your dieting friend is easing towards the refrigerator.

Sometimes it warns of something more serious. The con artist. The school bully. The date rapist.

With practice, you can learn how to sort out that feeling of warning from other types of unease. Once you have this skill down, it's very hard to fool you unless:

- you're not paying attention, or
- you want to be fooled.

Listening to your gut can keep you safe from mischief, from fraud or theft, from violence.

Psychic empathy can also be used to build harmony and accord with people around you.

While psychic empaths cannot force people to feel a certain way, projective empaths can (whether consciously or unconsciously) radiate an energetic field of emotion to fill the space around them creating a space where people are more likely to feel happy (or sad or giddy). A radiant empath can literally create and go to "her happy place" – and can take you along for the ride.

Next, an empath, especially a radiant empath, can be better at nurturing than most people around her. She can create that "happy space" noted above, where people feel not only happy, but safe, respected, and loved. She's more aware of negative or unhappy feelings, and is therefore in a better position do something to resolve them. She can make a closer emotional connection, increasing that feeling of emotional intimacy. She can be good at helping people to feel valued and loved, and at building good self esteem.

When an empath is happy, compassionate and in control of her gift, she can make the world a beautiful loving place for all of the people around her.

Empathy not only gives you better understanding of people around you. It also improves your ability to communicate with them, and helps them communicate with you.

As an empath, if you pay attention to emotional input, people around you are not only speaking to you with their words, but also with their emotional vibrations. You can "read between the lines" and hear what they're not saying, as well as what they actually say.

This can be a mixed blessing. You can use that unspoken information to help to better connect with them, but it's impolite to blatantly rub their noses in the unspoken dialog. No one likes to be told what they are feeling by someone else. If another person chooses to mask their feelings, you must treat that with respect. The empath receives more information than most people do, and the price of that is using it courteously and discretely. If not, you alienate the person you're trying to connect with.

The psychic empath can tell from emotional energy when a conversation is going well, and when things are not. She can perceive negative energy that tells her this is a touchy topic; she's gone too fast or been too blunt; or that she may need to try from a different angle.

The radiant empath can communicate with words, and also on an unspoken emotional level, perceived by empaths and non-empaths alike. She can create a field of positive energy supporting more accord and co-operation, as well as better communication.

The empath is also good at what I call "translation"- not language to language but rather between two people at odds who cannot see the common ground between them (and there is almost always common ground to be had...). She's good at showing parties in conflict where they agree; breaking down barriers between them.

Given these communication skills, an empath can also be an asset in negotiations. She can tell when both parties have found compromises that they can live with; and also when someone's saying the result is fine, but doesn't really feel that way. (Something that usually leads to more conflict later along...) Because she translates well, she's good at bringing people together.

When you have two or more sides in conflict, an empath is a true asset in bringing those sides together.

And, saving the best for last, psychic empathy makes it easier to share the joy. Know how miserable it is when negative emotions are battering on your energetic door? Well, there's a flip side to this...

When people are happy...

When people are curious...

When people are exuberant...

You get to share in the fun.

For the empath, people's emotions are contagious, positive or negative. When they're happy, you get to share that good time. Ever been in a situation where someone gets giggly and silly, everyone around them catches it, and you all laugh 'til tears pour down your faces? It's like that.

If people are having a good time, you can ride along on

their energy. If people are calm and serene, you can also hit that Zen point with far less effort. And if people are drinking, you can get a bit tiddly without drinking a drop...

Remember back in chapter six on shields, I said there might be times when you might want to decrease the level of your shields or drop them altogether? This is what I was talking about, a safe occasion where you lower your shields so you can enjoy emotional energy around you. What you want to consider in such a situation is:

- Is the emotional energy around you pleasant?
- Is it something you would like to experience?
- Is there too much energy? Even if it is pleasant, is it so much that it might overwhelm you?
- Is it likely to change rapidly? Is there emotional drama in the situation that might cause it to change quickly from good to bad?
- Is the situation safe for you to be affected by the emotional energy of others? (Ex: if your friend is drunk and happy, and you're the designated driver, controlling the emotional energy you're open to is as key as control of the alcohol you drink...)

Good judgment in this context is important for having a good time without letting it go wrong on you.

The radiant empath can share the joy in another way. He can take in positive energy, and reflect it back out to the world, magnified. This helps people around him feel even better, creating an upward spiral of emotion.

This upward spiral is great normally, but excels in the performing arts. The basic technique of projecting emotion as part of a performance makes the show better, but when performer and audience build an upwards spiral of mutual appreciation, the result can be magical.

It took time and effort to gain control of your gift. Since you have, it's fun to share the love with other folks. Now your gift is a true gift. You can make good use of it- do things that let you:

- Communicate better;
- Achieve your goals;
- Build harmony around you;
- Help others;
- Be safer;
- And have a lot of fun (amongst other things…)

This chapter paints a picture in broad strokes of some of many things you can do with your empathic gift. It's up to you to fill in that picture of how you want to use it. There are lots more options. Just think about it….

You've worked hard to learn what you need to do to own your gift, as opposed to letting it own you. The reward is a psychic gift that lets you make your world better.

The next chapters are for people around the empath:

- Co-workers and supervisors;
- Parents;
- Teachers;
- Friends;
- Lovers.

We'll look empaths in different roles, and how people around the empath can understand and support her.

These chapters are written mostly for non-empaths. Empaths may want to read them, too. You may learn something you hadn't understood before. And, if you're an empath who works with, loves, or is raising an empath, being one yourself doesn't mean you automatically "get" the experience of your fellow psychic.

On to the next chapter, on working with the empath.

Fourteen
The Empath at Work

What if you're not an empath yourself? What if you work with one, or live with one, or are raising one, or are in love with one? How do you make that work? What do you need to do to make that work?

We're going there next.

These next three chapters were not written primarily for the psychic empath (though they may be useful to one who wants to help a <u>fellow</u> empath). They're for the person who works with an empath. The person raising one. The person with an empathic friend. The person who loves one.   These chapters are written to help you support your empathic associate, be it partner, child, friend, or lover.

In these chapters, I'm going to talk about signs and symptoms of the psychic empath observable by the average person, psychic or not. Since empaths vary, both in strength of gift and amount of control, what you see in your personal empath may vary widely from what's described here. Keep in mind that I'll be talking about some of the more extreme signs of an empath- one with little control. (Indeed, these symptoms can even be those of an empath unconscious of her gift). With more control of his gift, he may be free of some or all of the limitations that I'll be describing.

I'm going to show you how to support the empath in your life. To do that, we're going to start by talking about working with a psychic empath.

For starters, how do you know if you're working with an empath? Some possible signs of this are a co-worker who:

- Seems sensitive or easily stressed;
- May have a larger personal space than average;
- Is the office "momma" or problem solver;

- Is more likely to get sick in times of stress;
- Is good at running meetings;
- Is subject to burn-out;
- Is good at negotiating compromises;
- Is more likely to need "alone time" at work;
- Reacts to a cold word from a person as if that person is yelling loudly at him;
- May be intensely "touchy-feelie" or else not "touchy-feelie" at all;
- Becomes cranky when other people are cranky (or anxious, or giddy…);

These characteristics are indicative of psychic empathy, but are not definitely conclusive evidence of it. Any of these behaviors may appear in a person with no psychic ability whatsoever, let alone empathy. The more of these points your co-worker exhibits though, the more likely it is that he or she has at least a touch of empathy. (By report, empathy is the type of psychic ability most frequently found in the general population.)

Having a co-worker who's a psychic empath can be wonderful. When your empath co-worker is happy, he'll do a great job of making sure that everyone around him is happy too. But, your empath cubicle mate may need to do things a bit differently from most people to stay on the happy side of the job.

And you can help him out with that….

If you're working with a psychic empath, what's the best thing you can do for him or her? Stay calm. Or better yet, try to consistently be as positive as possible for you at any particular moment.

Unless you're working with an empath with good shields and energy management skills, your emotional energy (and everyone else's…) is going to have an effect on him. The more energy there is to manage, and the more volatile the emotions are, the more metaphorical torches he'll be juggling in mid-air.

Too much energy, and he may have a melt-down (and since emotional energy is an unlimited resource, every empath, no matter how together he is, will sooner or later reach "too much").

If you keep yourself cheerful and mellow, you'll be easier for him to be around and work with. Indeed, if you can maintain that mellow, you can actually become an energetic still point that helps him roll with the energy of other more dramatic people in your workplace.

And, at times when you find yourself in a fractious mood you cannot work yourself out of, you may want to put some space between you to give him some insulation. You have to work together, but that's a great time to communicate online or by phone, do some visits out of the office, or go out to lunch. Even pushing your chair a foot over so your energy fields aren't overlapping can help.

Keep calm; and know your efforts will pay off for you in a better work partner and situation.

The psychic empath is sensitive to emotional vibrations. If he doesn't have control of his empathy yet, this can be distracting/overwhelming to him. Touching another person makes him even more sensitive to these vibrations. In compensation, the empath may try (consciously or unconsciously) to build in a little extra space between him and other people.

He may have a larger personal space, standing further away from people than usual. He may try to place himself so there's a wall, corner or empty space on at least one side of him, as it gives him an area free of empathic input. If a number of people share an open room for office space, he may try to grab the desk on one wall or in the corner, or create an artificial cubicle almost like a nest for himself using file cabinets or other office furniture. He may position his desk facing the wall (when the empathic sensory center in his abdomen/solar plexus is facing a "no energetic input" area, it decreases surplus empathic vibrational distractions as he works.)

How can you help with this? Give him his space...

- Don't get in his face or crowd him when talking to him.
- Don't touch him unless he invites you to, or iniates contact in some other way.
- Be aware if he takes a step back, so you don't unconsciously take a corresponding step forwards.
- In a meeting full of people, adjust your position so you're not pressed up against him.
- Don't insist that he rides in an elevator already packed full of people. There'll be another one along in a minute
- Let him sit on the end of the row in an auditorium, or let him put his belongings on chairs on either side of him, so that he can create some artificial space.
- Let him have the desk in the corner, against the wall, or in the cubicle, if he wants it.

The examples listed here apply to the more extreme symptoms of the empath in the workplace. Your situation will vary, dependant on the strength of his gift and how much control he has of it. The results can be anything from the near claustrophobic behaviors noted above to a very mild "touchiness".

Whether your empath has complete control of his gift or is at the mercy of every little emotional wind that blows, things like those listed above can make managing his gift at work and his life overall much easier. This leaves him free to be a better co-worker to you.

So everybody wins..

Speaking of space, you should know that, in many workplaces, personal space overlaps. Emotional drama in your cubicle, which backs on an empath's cubicle, means he'll end up carrying the weight of that energetic input like a psychic version of second hand smoke.

If you need to talk trash with a co-worker, help your empath out by taking it down the hall....

The vibrational input of a workplace can be overwhelming to the psychic empath; and because it's a job, the empath can't just walk away when he needs to. He may need to find ways to take professionally appropriate "alone time" to ground out negative energy, strengthen his positive vibrations, and do the vibrational maintenance needed for the empath at work.

A bathroom break to ground out negative energy while washing his hands. A lunch out doing errands, to separate from the work place energy. A coffee break in the car or other private space, to regain his center.

It's not that he's anti-social if he doesn't eat lunch with other employees, or chooses not to go out for a drink after work. He may just need "alone time" to manage the emotional vibrations he experiences. The "on the job" empath will work as hard as any other employee or even harder, but he may need to make time to separate himself from workplace energy.

When talking to the psychic empath, it's good to remember that he not only hears the words you're saying, but also what you're really feeling about those words and about him as well. This means that it's difficult to deceive him, and it's best to be compassionate but honest with him.

If you're feeling angry or stressed, you'll get better results if you can get your own head on straight and calm down before you give him directions. You can literally be talking quietly with your mouth while screaming at him with your spirit. In situations where emotions run extra high, if you cannot calm down, it may work better to give the empath his directions in writing, as opposed to creating an emotionally charged situation for him to deal with If you can't cool yourself off, he'll get the burden of your negative emotions together with your directions, whether those feelings were about him or not.

He'll do far better on the job if you give him feedback, as opposed to only criticism. A positive attitude, clear and honest directions from you, and the chance to use the feedback to improve will give you the best chance of getting what you want from him in his work. Harsh criticism with only negative input will overwhelm him emotionally, and sabotage any chance of improvement before it's begun. Compassionate feedback will support him energetically so that he has the energy to adapt to do what the job needs.

And the psychic empath working at full effectiveness is what everyone wants in the workplace.

Emotional sensitivity. Controlling your feelings so you don't affect his. Space. Alone time. Given all of the issues we've just gone through in this chapter, isn't a psychic empath just more trouble than he's worth? Why would you even want to work with a psychic empath?

There are several good reasons...

First, your average psychic empath, regardless of his control, will work really hard to see that people around him are happy. When they're happy, it's easier for him to be happy. And if you work with him, one of those people he's trying to keep happy will be you...

This means things like a positive workplace with extra good working conditions. People feeling respected and heard. Goodies brought in from home. Team work.

This also means positive attention to customers and clients. Great customer service. Job performance above and beyond what's required of an employee.

If he's a radiant empath, the whole mood of the part of the business he works in can become even more positive.

And all of this is good for business. As well as making your workplace a better place to be.

The psychic empath is good at supporting a positive work space...but there's more to him than that.

He can sometimes seem like a loner because he may need space to manage emotional energy. Despite this, the empath also usually has excellent people skills. He's good at communicating with people. At making people feel good about themselves. At resolving conflict. At creating positive experiences.

He's persuasive, and also a good listener.

So, if he has enough control over his gift, it's good to put the empath in people positions.

On top of making people happy and interacting well with people, empaths are good at negotiating compromises.

They feel when people are receptive to an option, and when they're really not ok with something, even if they say they are. They're good at translating the proposals of opposing sides, so that each side can understand what the other side is saying; and they use their empathic skills to help people find common ground between them, smooth out any negative energy, let people hear what their counterpart is saying, and find a resolution that everyone can live with.

In the workplace, to be successful, people need to be motivated to do the work and do it well. Motivation is something else the psychic empath is good at. Not only is he personally motivated to succeed, he is also good at tuning into his co-workers and identifying the specific points that bring out the best in them. Many times, people will want to do what the empath encourages them to do.

He's good at bringing out the best in people, and supporting them in feeling good about it.

The empath is also good at tuning in on what motivates a customer to buy or rent an item, or book a service. He's often good at selling things, with the proviso that he'll be far better at vending things that people want or can benefit from, than things they don't want or need.

So, when you want to get people moving, a psychic empath is the right person for the job.

The empath at work is a person with particular challenges. As his co-worker, you can support him so he can control his energetic input and keep his center; and an empath in control of his gift has a lot to give back to his co-workers and business.

Next, we'll move on to raising the empathic child.

Fifteen
Empathic Children

We've looked at the empath at work. Now let's look at a different situation- raising the young empath.

Many times, young empaths are seen as shy, "fussy", weird, non-social, or emotionally damaged, because their parents and the world around them don't understand that they have different needs and ways of processing things from a non-empathic child. Society's rejection of what's normal and appropriate for the child empath can be hurtful, and cause her to hide or deny her gift (which can cause problems for her later on in life.)

Parents and caregivers that understand and accept that an empath is different; that support her in developing control of her gift and learning to use it effectively get a young empath off to a great start. This can sustain her all of her life long.

So is your child a budding empath?....

How do you know if your child is an empath? Let's look at that.

Is Your Child a Psychic Empath?

1) Is your child very sensitive? Do people describe her as "oversensitive"?
2) Does she laugh and cry more easily than other children? Does she seem to have mood swings?
3) Is she very tuned in to the people's feelings?
4) Does she tend to carry extra weight around her middle?
5) Does she spend a lot of time "hugging" herself or with her arms folded across her stomach or chest?
6) Does she often get an upset stomach?
7) Is her stomach upset when something's wrong?

8) Does she have likes/dislikes for certain people she can't explain?
9) Does she know who's trustworthy and who's not?
10) Can she tell when someone's hurt or upset, even if there's no visible sign of it?
11) Is she frustrated when people say there's "nothing wrong"?
12) Do friends bring her their problems?
13) Is she the peacemaker or problem solver in her group?
14) Does she want to "fix" situations for people she likes?
15) Does she, at times, find people exhausting or draining?
16) When she's tired or sick, does she have less tolerance for being around people?
17) Is she uncomfortable in crowds?
18) When someone is upset but talking quietly, does she ask them to "stop yelling"?
19) Is her joy or misery contagious? If she's feeling something, do other people start to feel that way too?
20) Does she easily feel overwhelmed?
21) Is she shy? Does she like spending time alone?
22) Does her mood change to match the moods of children or adults around her?
23) Does her mood change to match the moods of people around her, even if she doesn't interact directly with them?
24) Does she avoid being touched? Or contrary wise, does she touch people a lot?

Just as in the adults' survey, there are many other reasons (such as shyness, compassion, anxiety, or even abuse) that your child might exhibit any of the behaviors listed above. You'll want to talk with your child and rule these other situations out, but the more of these symptoms she has, the more likely it is that your child is a psychic empath.

For a more concrete confirmation of psychic empathy, remember to look for the girdle of Venus in your child's hand, as explained in chapter 1. Check the dominant hand (the hand she uses the most) for the semi-circle at the base of the fingers that indicates an empathic gift.

Please note that you can even determine if an infant is empathic by checking her palm and observing how the emotions of people around her affect her.

If your child is an empath, she needs to learn the skills to manage emotional energy, just like any adult, but at her own age level. As her parent, you're responsible to help her do this, whether you're an empath yourself or not.

If you're not an empath, you can still help her to learn what she needs. You may find it easier if you find an empath to help you, (some things are easier for an empath to teach or explain.) but even without empathic support, you'll still be able to help her succeed with her gift.

When working with a child empath, you'll use many of the same methods used by adults. The main difference is using techniques and words appropriate to the child's age, age level, comprehension, and maturity. A three year old understands different things than an eight year old. An infant is going to have different understanding than a pre-adolescent. Each does best working at her level.

Even within age groups, there's a wide variety of behavior. One nine year old may be shy and withdrawn, another more centered and self assured. That has an effect on what each child is ready to deal with.

I'll make some suggestions here, but, as a parent, you know your child better than I ever could, and you're in the best position to see how your child's doing and whether she needs to go slower or is ready to move forward.

Help your child learn what she needs to know about her

empathy on her level of understanding and at her speed. Just like you'd teach her anything else.….

What's the role of mom or dad for a young empath?

The adult empath can look at this book, choose what options speak to him, and move ahead on his own schedule. The empathic child, dependant on maturity and age, can do some things, but may need help to do others.

That's where mom and dad come in. You may need to choose which exercises fit your situation and your child best. You may need to teach your child techniques. You may need to watch your child for signs that she's getting overwhelmed, and remind her to do her techniques. You may even have to do some of these techniques for her, until she's old enough to do them for herself. This can seem doubly tricky if you are not an empath yourself...

Don't worry. You'll do fine. Even if you're not an empath, you know when your child is over stimulated or overwhelmed by how she acts. Knowing what you do about psychic empathy from this book, you'll have more than enough tricks and tools to help her to find her own way.

Like any parent, you don't know everything about raising your child yet; but, like any parent, you'll learn about what your young empath needs by being her parent.

One of the best ways to tell if your empathic child is having problems is to observe her behavior. Some signs of energetic overload include:

- Getting very quiet, or talking loudly, nervously or inappropriately;
- Getting twitchy or irritable;
- Fidgeting:
- Having sudden emotional shifts;
- Moving away from people:

- Mirroring other people's emotions;
- Hiding;
- Avoiding being touched;

Like other things in this book, there are other possible reasons besides empathic overload for these behaviors, but watching for activity like this lets you know when your child needs help to regain empathic control.

Your child may need to strengthen her shields, ground out energy, or take some private time. By knowing her personal signs of overwhelm, you can help her take better control of her gift.

Learn the personal signs that your child needs help. Teach her those signs, so she becomes more aware of her own energetic state. Help her learn to manage her empathy.

One of the earliest ways to help a young empath deal with unwanted emotional energy is playing with water to ground it out. Washing her hands. Playing in the bathtub. Running under the sprinkler in her bathing suit in the summer time.

Start when your child's in a good mood, building good habits when it's easier. As water goes down the drain, teach your child to picture all of the "bad feelings" going with it. You might even have a special family rhyme or song about "washing the twitchies away" or "seeing your mad go down the drain". Praise her for doing a good job of "rinsing the yukkies away". A family ritual makes it easier to remember when your child's feeling overwhelmed. This is good to start when your child is young.

Even before this, you can use water to help the empathic infant. If your baby shows signs of empathic overload, you can use bath time to ground out negative energy. While bathing your child, set an intention (chapter three) for any negative emotional energy your baby has picked up to be released into the bathwater and go down the drain, to be recycled by the Earth. While it's wrong to use any technique to interfere with someone's free will, this is a good way to help a child too young, overwhelmed or disabled to help herself. You can use water for grounding from the moment you realize she is an empath.

There are other things that should start as young as possible but must wait until she's old enough to understand what you say. One of the most important is to learn that she is ultimately responsible for her own vibration....

Children growing up have a lot to deal with. They have to learn things in school, do chores, take care of their own hygiene, mind their manners, and work and play nicely with other children (and that's only to start with...)

Your young empath has more to deal with than the average child. She must deal with emotional energy around her, and, until she learns to manage energy, it'll push on her most of the time. It's easy to get angry, twitchy, cranky, or blue under the circumstances. Your young empath needs to know that, even if she's cranky because of the energy she's dealing with, she still owns that cranky and the results of it.

Empathy can be a burden before it's a gift. It's not fair, but that's how it is. If she lets empathy make her sullen or sad, she still ends up with the consequences of her moods and actions. The best gift you can give her is to not only teach her how to manage her empathy, but also that she's responsible for her own emotional vibrations, no matter what the energy around her is like.

If she ends up acting overwhelmed, angry, freaky or depressed, the world won't make allowances because she's an empath. It'll see her as who she becomes in response to the vibrations she experiences.

To have a happy and successful life, she needs to learn to take responsibility for her own vibrations as early as possible. She needs to:

- Be aware of signs that she is getting overwhelmed;
- Give herself voluntary "time-outs", to take a break from emotional input and regain her center;
- Use water or other methods to ground out negative, excessive, or stuck energy;
- Work on ways to maintain a positive energetic emotional set point (putting your "happy face" on);
- Control how much emotional energy she takes in;
- Learn how to shield herself;

And other such things. Just like an adult empath, but at her own level of comprehension, maturity, and ability. As her parent, you'll need to teach her these things, and also need to teach her to take responsibility for herself.

- Cueing her in to signs of oncoming overwhelm;
- Reminding her to ground;
- Asking her to either get her feelings under control, or take some quiet time in her room.

Teaching her how to become a happy, successful, well-adjusted adult. Just like any other parent does.

Besides grounding with water, responsibility for her own vibrations, and awareness of when she's approaching overload, one of the first things you need to teach your young empath is manners. That's right, manners - but a special type of manners, especially for psychic children.

Empaths can stand out from other children until they gain control of their gift. Some people may even see them as "weird" or "strange". Because of this, one of the first things an empathic child needs to learn is to keep her gifts private.

Some folks may wonder if this is dishonest, or means you're ashamed of the child's gift. It doesn't. If you think about it, there are many things (names and addresses, bodily functions, private family information, etc.) that we teach children to keep totally secret; or to only share with people approved by their parents, so they're used to things that are private. Keeping the fact that your child is psychic private will help her to fit into the world around her, which makes for a happier life.

Besides keeping the empathic gift a family secret, there are other facets of manners for psychics. One of them is not prying into the feelings of others. Just like adult empaths, children need to know that it's ok to perceive the surface emotions of others, but that it's not o.k. to pry deeper. Private means private. An empathic child also needs to know that it's o.k. to make an exception in a situation where her safety is in question. Even then, she should only probe deeply enough to stay safe.

Last, it's important for the empathic child to learn that sometimes people like to keep their emotions private, even if she can read their surface emotions. It's not ok for her to tell them how they really feel, if they are saying something different. This is frustrating to empaths (child and adult) but if people are hiding their feelings, they have a right to do so. At that point, it can be frustrating or unnerving for these people to have someone confront them with something that they're not ready to admit to.

Manners for the psychic child make it easier to fit into the regular world while she develops her gift, making for a happier childhood. Just like standard manners.

It's important for your child to learn to ground out unwanted energy as soon as she can. Many of the methods we used for adults are also workable at child-sized levels.

Besides using water, a child can ground by:

- Eating grounding foods;
- Taking deep breaths:
- Playing vigorously:
- Stomping, jumping, or dancing;
- Sitting and bouncing, or fidgeting;
- Hugging a tree;
- Or any physical activity.

At first, basic activity may be all the younger child can do. As she gets old enough, teach her to visualize negative energy draining away into the Earth to be recycled, making grounding more effective.

You may want to talk her through this at first, praising her for grounding energy and getting her center back. (Non- empathic parents can tell when this happens because the child becomes calmer and more focused, back to her normal self). As your child learns, she'll move to first only needing a reminder to ground, and then being able to do it independently, without parental intervention.

Just as many adult grounding activities can be "sized down" for kids, so can be methods of controlling how much energy they take in.

Their first and best choice is just not to be there when they realize that emotional energy is overwhelming. Leave if they can. Excuse themselves. Go to the bathroom. Take a personal time out. Whatever they can do to get out of the emotional overload, and to a place where they can ground out negative energy and get their center back. This is the same thing you'd teach a child about any dangerous situation – if you can, the best thing is to walk away.

But sometimes you can't leave. So, what next?

Other options include:

- Getting more space between you and the source of the emotion. Step back.
- Turning partially or fully sideways, so the empathic sensory center is not facing the emotional person. (Practice with your child so it looks more natural).
- Cross your arms over your chest or stomach.
- Or combine two or more of these (take a step back and turn slightly sideways.)

Remember caffeine and sugar can also help with overwhelming energy; but, as a parent, you'll probably want to have some control over that.

Practice options with your child when times are calm, so that when things become more exciting, they already have the techniques they need as good habits.

Once your child gets some basic empathic techniques

down, it may be time to start working on developing shields. Bedtime can be one good time for this.

Tell your child to close her eyes and picture herself surrounded by light, in a color she likes. Tell her to picture that light getting brighter and stronger, until she's totally safe in a little house made of light; and no one's feelings can come into her house unless she says ok. Tell her she has a peephole in the door of her little house of light, so she can look out, see what's there, and decide what she wants to let in and what she doesn't.

Another choice, if your child prefers it, is using images of force fields or magical shields from fantasy or anime stories.

Once is not enough to build her shields, but if this is part of your bedtime routine, she'll gradually develop the shields she needs to better manage the energy around her.

Meditation can be very useful for an empath. It's one way to ground out excess or negative energy and bring one's self back to center and to balance. A full meditation practice may be too much for a young child. Fortunately, there are simple ways to meditate that a child can do.

Simple breath work – focusing on your breathing as you breathe in and out, helps to calm and relax you. Teach a child to focus on her breathing, then gradually slow it down and relax as she does so. This can be a useful skill for a child in everyday life, as well as grounding of energy.

Watching clouds is another simple way of focusing, relaxing, and meditating. Look for clouds that look like something, or guess which way the cloud will move next.

Looking into a fire is great for calm, introspection and regaining your center. A child can do this looking at a camp fire, enclosed candle, or fire in the fireplace. Make it a game by setting a quiet timer and having them look for pictures in the flames. (No talking 'til the buzzer goes off).

Starting the young empath on beginning meditation gives her tools to regain peace for herself when the world is challenging.

As your young empath grows in confidence, skills, and control, you'll want to teach her more than how to defend her borders from unwanted energy. You'll want to teach her how to actively use her skills. She may figure some of this out, but any active training you do will help her to better tap into what's useful and fun about her gift.

Begin by learning how to feel different emotions when needed. Not faking emotion, but being able to choose to be happy, sad, or deceptive at will. Fans of method acting are already familiar with this.

Once your child has insight into managing empathic input, you can start making up games where the object is to identify the emotion without physical feedback (like words, facial expressions, or body language).Your job is to feel a random emotion. Your child's, to identify it by empathy.

This shouldn't be a test. Make it fun. Hide behind a screen and play "Name that Emotion". Use picture cards that stimulate an emotional response in you to play Empathic Concentration. Play Hide and Seek where you hide and project strong emotion to help your child find you.

Empathic parents can use radiant empathy to give children game cues. Parents who aren't empaths can still feel things deeply and change emotions when they choose, trusting their child to pick up what's happening. Making learning fun means everyone wins.

Finally, one way for empathic children to learn better control over their gift is to get into acting, singing, or other performing arts if they're interested. Theatre can teach an empath a lot about emotional energy, whether it's in the cast of a major production, or playing "dress-up" with your baby sister. When people play "let's pretend", they tend to experiment with emotions at a lighter setting. This is good practice for the young empath.

Audience response can also teach an empath about controlling radiant vibration, as well as the energy they take in. Any kind of make believe or performing art is a great classroom for your empathic child, if she's personally ready for and interested in it.

Each child is different, so you'll find not all of these ideas fit your young one. Watch for the signs of being overwhelmed we talked of earlier in the chapter to help you decide what's working and what's not. Keep in mind that a technique may work in some cases, and not others, and you may need more than one way for your child to thrive.

The bottom line is you'll have to customize and choose yourself what works for your young empath from techniques we've talked about, to give her what she needs. To learn, grow, thrive and be happy. Just like any parent...

Next stop – the empath up close and personal...

Sixteen
The Personal Touch -
Psychic Empaths as Friends or Lovers

If you're this far in the book, you know a lot about psychic empathy. You know both how to gain control of the gift and to use it once you have control. You know about empaths on the job and raising the young empath.

Now it's time to look at personal relationships. At friendship, and at love...

Many of the skills you'll need to be a good friend or loved one to an empath are in the two previous chapters. This chapter is about getting more deeply into skills you need for more personal relationships in life. Friends and lovers are two very different types of people, but the skills we'll talk about overlap over both kinds of relationships, differing mainly in a matter of degree).

Let's get started then. Are you an empath's friend or lover? Here's how you can help him.

What's the very best thing you can do to support the psychic empath you care about? It's to get a handle on your own emotional energy.

Unless your empath has good control of his gift, he'll be affected by your emotions. When you're happy, he'll tend to be happier. When you're depressed, he'll be blue. He'll be carrying his own emotions, and yours as well. This can be exhausting, even with positive feelings.

This is not to say that you're not permitted to have your own emotions. You certainly are; but if you want to be part of the solution as opposed to part of the problem while he's getting control of his gift, keeping your emotional energy in calm, centered, and positive ranges takes a major burden off of him, and makes it easier for his to do the work he needs to do to manage his psychic empathy.

It's also good to remember that, even after he gets more control, the emotions of people around him can still have an effect on him. If you're grumpy and out of sorts, he'll have to work harder to keep himself in a happy space.

This happens. Nobody's positive all of the time, and everyone has "cranky-grumpy" days. The point is knowing that this not only affects you, but him as well. If you're off, you can throw him off if he can't protect his emotional energy. At that point, he may react to you in a negative way, which tends to make you more "cranky-grumpy", and the situation rapidly spirals downwards and out of control.

As noted in a previous chapter, one of the empath's tools is maintaining a positive emotional set point - an empathic "default setting" of positive energy to defend against creeping negativity from the world around her. As friend or lover, you could learn from that. If you worked on having your own positive emotional set point, it'd make it much harder to get knocked into a negative space. Your energy would be more positive and pleasant for an empath to be around on a regular basis; and your emotional state would be healthier and more fun for you, as well.

So manage your stress. Chill out. And learn to live in your "happy place". And life will be better for you both.

"He knows if you've been bad or good, so be good for goodness' sake...."

Santa Claus may know how you've been behaving, but an empath knows how you're feeling. It's difficult to fool him (unless he wants to be fooled...) This means that when you're feeling off, your empath knows it.

He'll probably ask you if something's wrong. If you're feeling bad, but tell him there's no problem (to be polite or spare him the burden of your problems), you'll either cause him to doubt his perceptions, or else frustrate him because he knows something's wrong and he wants to help you "fix" or work through it, so you both can get back to a happy place again.

Either way, this causes more problems than it's worth. If you're feeling down, better to be honest with him.

Stop a moment and look at what's happening. If he's

picking it up, there's something going on that you need to deal with. You can do something about it, or not. If you can do something about it, you may or may not want his help with it.

If you can do something about it:

- If you want his help, please let him offer.
- If you need to deal with it yourself, tell him thanks for caring, but let him know that this is something you need to sort out for yourself.
- If it's something that will take time or that you need some time to complete, let him know that as well.

If it's something that you can't do anything about currently, tell him this.

If you don't know where the negative state's coming from, let him know that as well. Sometimes these cases of the "drive-by blues" come from air pressure, exhaustion, or random stress.

Just don't try to hide your blues. It doesn't work well.

While we're talking about this, let's talk about communication with the psychic empath.

An empath communicates not only on the verbal level and through body language, but also on the emotional energetic level. When you're talking with an empath, he hears the emotional subtext, as well as the words that you're actually saying.

This can sometimes mean that how he responds to you makes no sense, because he's reacting to your emotional energy, as well as your words and your actions. You may have to ask him to explain his reactions because he's not seeing things with the same senses you do.

The best approach to take to communication with the empathic psychic is to be honest. Not the brutal, "in-your-face" confrontation often misnamed "total honesty", but rather to be straight with him in an honest, but kind and respectful way. One of the best ways to do this is talk with him when you're both centered and on an even keel. Tell him about how you usually communicate under different conditions. Are your family habitual yellers, or do they rarely raise their voices? When stressed, do you need to talk things out immediately or do you need a cooling down period? Ask how he usually communicates, and what types of communication bother him. Find communication styles you can both live with (maybe he yells a little more and you a little less...)

Understanding how each other communicates is particularly important when you fight. It may seem to you like he's overreacting. The truth is that he's reacting to your energy, as well as your words and actions. You need to be aware of this so you can both "fight fair" and reach an understanding with each other.

One important thing for a friend or lover of an empath to remember is that touch increases the impact of emotional energy. In your relationship, this does a number of things.

- If the empath feels energetically overwhelmed, touch will make it worse, unless your emotional energy is extremely calm and centered.
- If you feel sad or angry, touch will pass that emotion right to him.
- And touch, whether a friendly pat on the back or something more adult oriented, tends to strengthen the relationship between you (for good or ill).

When an empath's having a hard time, it's a good idea to give him space, unless you have the calm and stable energy that can help him ground out him overwhelm.

It's also good to know that exhaustion, illness, or injury can decrease his control over his gift, leaving him more vulnerable to external emotions. If he's not feeling well and wants to stay home, there's a good reason for that.

We've talked about having control of your own emotions, and about developing a communication style that works for you both. What other ways can you support the empath you care about?

First, become more aware of what people, things, and experiences are more challenging for him.

- Are crowds hard for him to handle?
- Do certain people tend to blow him circuits?
- Does he have less control of his gift when tired or sick?

If you know that certain things are more likely to overwhelm him, you'll understand if he tends to avoid these things or be more irritable around them. If more than one of these happens at once, he's even more likely to be overwhelmed, and need to either withdraw or blow up.

Dependant on your relationship, you might ask if he wants you to alert him when he's heading for something challenging. If concentrating on something else, an empath sometimes overlooks this until he's in the thick of things. It's respectful to ask if he wants a heads up.

Speaking of overwhelm, things go better if you don't stack challenge upon challenge.

- Need to have a sensitive conversation? Don't have it in a crowded room.
- Need a favor from him? Don't ask him right after he gets off the phone with obnoxious aunt Mathilda.
- Want to go out dancing at a crowded club? He may not

want to after a nasty day at work.

Know that, if he has a challenging experience, she may need time to ground out and get back to center. Give him that space, and don't crowd him.

A third way of helping him is to know his own methods of coping with overwhelm, and supporting those.

- Does he have a comfort food that helps him ground and center? Be sure to have some in the house, or offer to go get some if needed.
- If he's in a challenging situation, does he need to leave (even if the event isn't over?) Be supportive. Don't make him feel guilty for spoiling your fun.
- Does he need to ground?
- If he's not realizing he needs to shield or ground, does he want a reminder or would that be pushing? (A point best settled in a calm and centered time, as opposed to in crisis.)
- If he'd like a reminder, what would be a respectful way to do this?
- One of the best ways I've heard this done is simply asking "How can I help?"
- Finally, once you've offered support, accept if it's something he needs to work out herself. Just as he needs to accept if you need to work out one of your negative moods.

After reading this chapter, does it seem like your empathic friend or lover is high maintenance? Well, he has different needs than the average bear, but he also has far more to offer.

The well balanced empath with good control of his gift can be a delightful person to have as a friend or lover. He cares about people around him, and works hard to nurture, heal and delight them. He's great at making any place that he is the happy place. He'll know when you're down and help boost you back up.

And, if you support his use of his gift, you both can build an upwards spiral of good feelings and good times that nurture you both.

Value your empath for what he is, and relax into the sunshine of his love.

Seventeen
One Journey Ends; Another Begins

It's been a long journey from the out of control psychic empath to the empath whose gift is truly a gift to her and the world around her.

We've talked about what it means to be an empath. About shields and ways to control energetic input, and to cut it off, if needed. About grounding out negative energy. About knowing whether energy belongs to you or someone else; and about keeping your own energy positive, to repel negative energy.

We've talked about the bright side of being an empath, and positive things you can do with your gift once you have control of the effects of energy on you

We've talked about the empath at work. About raising the young empath. About empaths as friends and lovers, and how people around them can support the empath they care about. We've gone through lots of concepts, techniques, and tools.

And now, it's all up to you.

While psychic empaths share the same gift, they're all still unique individuals. One empath will like certain techniques, and another prefer different ones. That's why I've given you such an assortment of ways to manage your gift to choose from.

It's not enough to have the contents of this book, though. To make your gift work for you, you first need to work with the techniques. Play with them. Find which ones are most natural and positive for you.

You need to practice them. Build empathic habits. Make them routine until they become automatic – until you can deal with whatever energy comes to you.

And then, you reap the rewards of the gift of psychic empathy....

This book is over...but your own journey has just begun.

And I hope this book will be a guide, and a help, and a companion on your journey of discovery – the journey to becoming the empath that you were born to be.

I wish you joy…

I wish you peace…

I wish you the kind of empathic gift that makes
your world a wonderful place…

And, most of all, I hope that you find what you need to
make your gift most practical for you.
That you become a practical empath.

Catherine Kane

Catherine Kane is a psychic empath, Reiki Master / teacher, professional psychic, bard, artist, wordsmith and songwright, enthusiastic Student of the Universe, maker of very bad puns, and overachiever (amongst other things...)

She loves empowering people to find and live their best and brightest dreams. Psychic empathy is one of the tools she uses to do this.

Currently, Catherine is once more setting forth on another literary adventure. Her next book she has planned is a practical guide to manifestation magick. She is also at work on a series of urban fantasy novels, which incorporate how energywork and magick work.

Her first book "Adventures in Palmistry" is available through www.ForesightYourPsychic.com and at her personal appearances. (For a list of events to see her in person, please see her website.)

Visit Catherine, and husband Starwolf as Foresight at
www.ForesightYourPsychic.com ,
www.ForesightYourCTPsychic.wordpress.com ,
or on Facebook at
www.facebook.com/pages/Foresight/172408108291

Also by Catherine Kane

Adventures in Palmistry

Your Destiny is in your hands -- and you can have a hand in your destiny! Reading palms can empower and enlighten you, giving you the information you need for the adventure of life, and enabling you to help others around you. And it can be a lot of fun, as well. "Adventures in Palmistry" makes palmistry easy and fun. It will put the power of palmistry in your hands.

For more information, please visit Foresight Publications at www.ForesightYourPsychic.com

CPSIA information can be obtained at www.ICGtesting.com
Printed in the USA
LVOW12s1337080215

426174LV00001B/360/P

9 780984 695195